YOUR END OF THE BOAT IS SINKING

by
Barbara Bayley

author of "I Could Always be a Waitress"

Copyright © 2013 Barbara Bayley
All rights reserved.

ISBN: 1492717878
ISBN 13: 9781492717874

Dedication

For my granddaughter, Jenni, without whose invaluable computer skills this book would never have been published – Thank You, with Love!

Your End of the Boat is Sinking

Back in the early 1970s I wrote a few articles and sent them to our local newspaper, the Melbourne <u>Times</u>. I was in the right place at the right time: Weona Cleveland, one of their columnists and community historian, needed surgery and I was hired as a temporary replacement for her.

I loved being allowed to write whatever I wanted on any subject, and my subjects were my family (not always willing) and the community (like the lady who didn't like the car she had bought, so drove to the office in her vehicle that she had covered in yellow plastic lemons). My job lasted only a couple of weeks, but by then I had printer's ink in my veins and six months later, after much more freelance writing sent to editor Lucille Kahn (*Me: "How is my writing?" Lucille: "You have a knack for writing about anything and everything." Me: "But do you have any criticism?" Lucille: "Well, you do tend to scatter commas like confetti."*) I was given a column of my own.

I titled it "Your End of the Boat is Sinking", because I loved John Donne's quote that "no man is an island unto himself" — so I hope for you that my book represents this idea: that if we float or sink, we cannot take the credit alone.

All the stories and anecdotes are true.

Especially the dreams.

Barbara Bayley
2013

Your End of the Boat is Sinking

Chapters

1	Famous People who will be Glad they met me, like Richard Chamberlain	1
2	Joe Namath Opens a Drugstore in Palm Bay	7
3	632 Arch Street, New Britain, Connecticut	13
4	There is a Tavern in the Town	21
5	Tales from Behind the Funeral Home	29
6	Aluminum and Wrought Iron	33
7	Going—Going—Gone!	39
8	The Painter of Mustard and Ketchup	47
9	Ya Load Sixteen Tons and Here's What Ya Get	51
10	All the News that's Fit to Sit	57
11	The Store on the Corner	61
12	The Girl who Loved Box-ing	65
13	Their Dancing Daughters (and Sons)	69

14	To Work or Not to Work? That is the Question (for Women Back Then)	71
15	PROOF OF GOD AND HIS/HER SENSE OF HUMOR	75
16	All Roads Meet in Ocala	79
17	Titusville Dream	83
18	Losing Chris	87
19	The One-Armed Woman with the BB Ashtray	91
20	The Good Fairies of the Episcopal Church in Orlando	97
21	It's Very Quiet in the Sky When the Plane Runs Out of Gas	99
22	Jon and His Unworn Knees	105
23	How Did She Get Past Security With That?	111
24	Racing with the Moon	113
25	Animal Quackers	115
26	Monkey Business	123
27	I Run Away to Join the Circus	127
28	Organ Notes	131
29	Miscellaneous Musings	137
30	Ending with a Laugh	175

Your End of the Boat is Sinking

I was chatting recently with a neighbor about a high school summer job I had once, looping springs.

"How many jobs have you *had*?" she asked. So I started counting and then realized that each of these jobs has its own stories. So here's the list; the (*all true*) stories follow:

Before I went to college I was paid to be a

- sock ironer
- babysitter
- piano accompanist for a children's dance studio
- piano accompanist for a ritzy private high school
- Girl Scout helper at a day camp
- storm window seller over the phone
- steel strapping inventory person
- spring looper
- cashier at a very fancy restaurant
- organist at church.

Jobs since majoring in American Literature at college:

- wife and mother (I was paid in room and board and benefits—the I.R.S. Does not recognize this as a paying job)
- waitress at an Italian restaurant
- Staff writer, Melbourne Times newspaper
- Licensed Mental Health Counselor
- organist
- choir director
- piano teacher

- playwright
- instructor of Women's programs at Brevard Community College
- dental office manager and all-around assistant
- keyboard player of the "Has-Beens" combo.
- and I have to add a winning anecdote that was published in "Reader's Digest".

Stick around—there's more....

Famous People who will be Glad they met me, like Richard Chamberlain

(This is not a job—just so you know I will throw in other stuff from time to time:)

If you agree that the end justifies the means, then I am proud of this story.

If not—at least you will know with whom you are dealing. (I was an American Lit major with an English minor at Boston University, so I know not to finish a sentence with a preposition—I just don't know why not to.)

The <u>Monty Python</u> TV shows were part of my early adult years, along with <u>Mad</u> magazine and <u>Pogo</u>. So when I read that Richard Chamberlain was coming to Melbourne, Florida as the King in Monty Python's "Spamalot", I hurried to be one of the first to buy a ticket.

On opening night—here in Melbourne, Florida! Richard Chamberlain! The "Thorn Birds" guy!—I sat in the balcony and laughed my way through the show. At the end of the second act a henchman even came off the stage into the audience and chose someone to come up onstage and be the Peasant of the Year with the chalice. That night it was a very old lady who could hardly climb the stairs.

There was no rewind button to a live show, so I bought another ticket immediately. It would be on the next night, the night before my 72nd birthday, and I wanted to sit as close as I could this time, to catch every nuance and joke. I was able to get a single seat downstairs about 12 rows back, on the aisle. What a great birthday gift!

The next night I found my seat and looked around. Right up front way ahead of me on the right aisle was a *single seat*! Oh, why hadn't I reserved *that* one? I watched to see if anyone would claim it, but nobody did.

Now for family and friends who have never thought of me as devious, prepare to be educated:

I needed a plan if I was to get to that seat after intermission. My goal was to get as close to the stage as possible; but I knew the ushers to be a hardened group who would give even Navy Seals a tough time if they wanted to change seats.

So—what reason could I give that would keep an usher from questioning my excuse? I took a chance and at intermission approached a female usher about my age.

"I hate to bother you," I said, almost in a whisper, "but there's a man sitting near me and he's wearing cologne that's just making my eyes water."

That was Step One.

"He's also been drinking, I think, so he's a little smelly."

Okay, Step Two.

And my Step Three clincher—"He also doesn't seem to have bathed in a few days, and the odor is really getting to me." I was taking the chance that although she might squint her eyes at me about the cologne and the drink, she wouldn't dare go up to him and check out his body odor.

"So I wondered if I might take that seat in the second row, on the end. No one has been sitting in it."

Why all the subterfuge? I dealt in personality types as a therapist and I knew that the type of personality an usher has does *not* like change of any kind and does not want to back down. I wanted to give her a way to say "Yes" that would save her sense of right and wrong. I figured if I approached her head-on she'd deny me. And she, not I, had the Power of The Seat Assignment.

She looked toward that coveted seat and then back at me. I smiled at her. Come on, my smile said—what can you fear from a gray-haired woman like me? "It's also my birthday tomorrow," I added, ready to pull out my driver's license just in case. Then I stopped talking. Maybe the birthday bit was overkill.

Now she pulled the Change Of Command bit on me. "Well," she said, "I'll have to go ask the head usher." And she headed off.

Now, I lied plenty as a kid—what kid didn't? — and I'd hoped I could get an answer before I lost my nerve. Only the thought of sitting in that second row seat kept me from blurting out, "No, never mind! You got me! I give up!", and slinking with a red face back to my old seat.

Uh oh—I could see that the head usher looked like a no-nonsense well-muscled woman. She'd get me to confess in short order.

My usher returned. "She says you can have it if nobody else sits there by the time the curtain goes up."

"Oh, thank you," I said with relief. The usher looked at me with the kind of suspicion that makes a young girl stammer and put her hands behind her back.

"He really *smells*? Funny nobody else has complained."

"I must have a very sensitive nose," I said, hoping mine was not growing.

I grabbed the seat and fell into it to claim my territory. A well-dressed Yuppie couple (who both smelled expensive) next to me glowered, "*You* weren't here before." I didn't answer.

The curtain went up on act 2. I was so *close*! Richard Chamberlain was right there in front of me! And then he asked for the chalice, the Holy Grail. The actors looked around and the henchman said something like, "I think I know where it is," and came down off the stage.

Now here is where my amateur theatrical training went into automatic: I noticed people around me looking at the stage, while **I** stared at the man coming toward me, and I smiled as big a smile as I could, looking him full in the face.

And oh thank you Lord, he grinned back at me.

"Here's the peasant with the chalice!" he yelled, and pulled me from my cherished seat up onto the stage and face to face with the King! King Richard! King Chamberlain!

Impulsively I went down on my knees and bowed, all my years with the Indian River Players coming back to me; and as I knelt before the King, realized to my horror that I couldn't get back onto my feet without grabbing at someone or something. I glanced out at the audience. With the lighting, I couldn't see anyone at all out there, but I could hear the roar of laughter—surely for me the most satisfying sound in the world next to a newborn baby's cry.

The King, a surprised look on his face ("Has this old gray-haired lady fainted?"), helped me up. We smiled at each other. Someone took a Polaroid photo of me with the cast, handed me a plastic award shaped like a golden foot, along with a paper that announced I was "Peasant of the

Year" and the photo, still developing, and hustled me back to my seat. My audience with the King, so well choreographed except for my bow, could not have taken more than a minute.

The couple next to me stared, eyes narrowed in unison. "You're a **shill**, aren't you?" one hissed. I shook my head and looked back at the stage, the stage I'd just been on, just been on!—, me, acting, acting with Richard Chamberlain, Richard Chamberlain, who was probably gay, but who cared, it was Richard *Chamberlain*!

I had the photo enlarged. I was at a store buying a frame for it when a woman stopped me. "I saw you at the show," she said. I nodded and held up my photo. "That was all set up, right?"

"No," I said. "I didn't know I was going to be called."

"But you weren't scared," she insisted. "I would have been *petrified*."

I couldn't tell her I'd already done some acting that day. And to the unknown man who originally sat near me—apologies. I'm sure you didn't really have body odor.

Onstage with Richard Chamberlain.

Joe Namath Opens a Drugstore in Palm Bay

"Pro football is like nuclear warfare.
There are no winners, only survivors."
Frank Gifford, <u>Sports Illustrated</u>, July 4, 1960.

Drive to the shopping center on the southeast corner of Babcock Street and Palm Bay Road in Palm Bay, Florida, and you will find a dollar store.

Formerly this store was an Eckerd's Pharmacy. The original familiar green-patterned terrazzo floor is still there, many years after another company bought the chain out and Mr. Eckerd retired.

If I go with you, I can point to The Very Spot where Joe Namath, the great-looking quarterback with the bedroom eyes, old Broadway Joe, and I went eyeball to eyeball.

I was working then as a staff writer for the Melbourne <u>Times</u>, a proud Melbourne area newspaper that had been reduced to a publication twice a week by the onslaught of the Gannett people from Rochester, New York, who brought <u>Florida Today</u> to Brevard County around 1967. Melbourne reeled from the printers' punch and never recovered.

I was fortunate to be there in the <u>Times</u>' last glory days, even wrote a column that my editor without my knowledge submitted to a statewide competition, and which, to my surprise, took a second place in a Florida newspaper with our circulation.

I was allowed to write about anything I wanted to; and *I* wanted to write about Joe Namath. We were fervently into the age of Equal Rights for Women, and we females bristled at any man taking advantage of us, especially a gorgeous dark-haired guy like this Joe Whoever. This is my Times column:

Joe Willie "Mr. Broadway" Namath, the professional football quarterback, the man with the dazzling smile and the hair you'd love to rumple, is coming to Palm Bay to help open Eckerd's newest pharmacy.

All I know about Joe is that he catches a ball well, runs well, is quite the ladies' man, and is willing to wear nylons in order to sell cologne on TV.

"*That's* your angle?" asks sportswriter Shelby Strother, leaning over my typewriter at the Times. Shelby, a walrus-mustached good-natured rumpled bear of a man in a Key West shirt, knows *everything* about sports. If I became his writing student I would learn how to put sentences together so beautifully that readers would laugh and then weep from one word to the next. But now, in 1976, I am too full of Women's Liberation to want to ask him humble questions about such a totally-male dominated sport.

"So, Barb—you know what team Namath plays on?"

"Uh—"

"You know where he went to school?"

"Well, uh—"

"You know what position he plays?"

"Well, Shelby, you're *supposed* to know those things," is the best I can do. I decide I will stick close to him so I don't look stupid. That way I can defer to him if anyone asks me a tough question like, "What's overtime?"

We drive together to Palm Bay. There's a crowd of a hundred or so excited people at the drugstore, lined up to get a close-up look at Broadway Joe himself and maybe grab an autograph.

And there he is! He's standing in the back of the store near the baby diapers and heat rash ointments, already smiling away and signing photos of himself. His blue eyes are twinkling as though he'd rather do this any day than play football. Two gorilla-like men watch the mob closely as if they are guarding the President. Despite myself, I'm impressed with his folksy manner toward his sweaty eager fans.

Well, of course he's used to sweat, I tell myself. He's a football player. However, he looks as though he could run the entire—how many?—uh, yards—I know that one!—without ever mussing his hair or smelling bad.

A woman turns back to me. Her sixty-year-old body is quivering like a young puppy's. "It looks just *like* him! She exclaims. "Just *like* him!"

This line is so good I jot it down in my notepad. "And," she continues, "he's *taller* than I thought he'd be!"

Her husband snorts, pulling in his stomach, thinking nobody has caught him doing this. "Huh. *I'd* look that tall if I was sitting on a wallet with all his money."

I have to admit Joe Willie Namath is lookin' good. He's kissing babies like a well-oiled politician, and even chastely kissing the good-looking young women as they hold their blushing cheeks out to him. I'm so close I can catch a whiff of his cologne. Wow, he smells good! Well, of course—he's here to tout his aroma, which Eckerd's will carry.

I need to buy some for my husband, I think, too mesmerized to take notes. I catch Shelby's eye. He's laughing at me. I frown at him to show that I am, after all, a serious reporter.

Joe is wearing a brown plaid shirt, open at the throat; tight-fitting jeans; black suede shoes; and a leather belt which reads "Rolls Royce". Well-toned muscles ripple beneath that clothing, His firm rear end has been patted by many men on the field and probably many women off the field.

He's trying to shake hands with the men now. He doesn't get a chance—women are flinging themselves at him for a hug and he willingly obliges.

"Give him your hand, Beau," says a young blonde-haired mother with a chubby tow-headed toddler in her arms. The boy, who has had most of his hand in his mouth, pops it out and offers Joe a very wet finger. Joe shakes it seriously.

His two bodyguards don't smile. They're not paid to smile.

In an hour I've turned from cynic into groupie. As he gets ready to leave, I push my way to his side. "Mr. Namath," I stutter, "will you please autograph a photo for my son?"

Now that dazzling smile is directed full at me. He must know some wonderful dentist! Vaguely I hear Shelby's guffaw from (it seems) far way. Those blue eyes are riveted on my brown ones.

"Well, certainly," he says. "What's your son's name?"

My son's name—my son's name—I am not kidding you when I say that I have forgotten the names of not just one, but *both* sons

"Uh—Barbara," I stammer, blushing. At least I still know my *own* name. Joe actually winks at me and signs a photo, writes my name on it and hands it to me.

Oh, I can't let him go yet! "Mr. Namath," I call as he moves away from me, his bodyguards flanking him the way the—uh, fullbacks?—must do on the field, "I'm writing an article about you for our newspaper. May I send you a copy?"

He turns back to me then and I feel the full force of his blue eyes on me. He grabs my arm and pulls me to him so that I am closer to his face than I usually get to my own husband's. He smells like Brut.

His gorgeous eyes flash like stars into mine.

"*No,*" he says.

I have never had a more memorable refusal.

A postscript in 2013:

I shop at the Publix that's almost next-door to that old Eckerd's store. I still have a wave of nostalgia when I enter the dollar store. "Don't you want to know what happened here once?" I want to call to the customers.

"What's your next book?" asks Diane, my grocery cashier.

"Well, it'll be a series of anecdotes. Like the time I met Joe Namath..."

The young woman bagging groceries looks up idly. "Who's Joe Namath?" she asks. "I never heard of him."

✫ ✫ ✫

Leslie Rackliffe in the National Guard.

632 Arch Street, New Britain, Connecticut

November, 1941 - I am three years old. I scale the side of baby Tommy's bassinet in the kitchen and I peer inside. There's a baby in there and Mommy is changing him. I stare. I'm not **built** like him! Is something the matter with me or with him?

We don't talk about these things.

1942 - I am sitting under the lilac bush in the front yard, on Arch Street. The boy from across the street is sitting cross-legged with me and he is teaching me how to whistle. I"m still good at it over 70 years later.

In our back yard is a cherry tree. We live in an enormous (to a four-year-old) three-story yellow house with green trim. It's beautiful. When I grow up I will discover that it's a Queen Anne.

We live on the first floor with Daddy's parents, my grandfather and Alo. Some cousins live upstairs and the third floor is where Uncle Howard lives. Howard paints and raises snakes and one day when cousin Jane is hanging out clothes from the second-floor window, a snake drops onto her head.

My sister Judy is a year and a half younger than me. I have to watch her, or she'll go out in the street naked, like she did once. Judy and I go to the house behind us. Its color is green and two old ladies live there, so we call them the Green Ladies. They always have coloring books for us to use when we visit them.

A little girl my age drowned in the brook near my house. I am warned never to go near that brook. That's my first fear of water.

My second one is when we are at The Shore and Daddy takes Judy and me out to a sandbar. He has one of us cradled in each arm and he stumbles a little on some shells. I am terrified—if he has to save one of us, I am *positive* it will be Judy and not me!

(Years later, as a mental health counselor, I am at a workshop where professionals are doing hypnosis and regression therapy. I let myself be hypnotized: I am on a boat with my father. I have a round head and I am wearing a bright yellow slicker. I am saying over and over again to him, "Why did you let me drown?")

September, 1942 - I'm in kindergarten. I walk up Arch Street and turn the corner and it's a block away. I learn how to cook Wheatena and to sew a brown oilcloth gingerbread man with yarn, in and out of the holes that the teacher has punched into the pattern.

During the year we are divided in two, and half of us go to sit with the first-graders while the other half takes a test; then we switch. The desks and seats are big enough for two children, and I sit and watch the work that my seatmate is doing. I get scared.

"I'll never make it through first grade!" I think.

Actually, this becomes my watchword—"If I made it through first grade, I can make it through most anything"—it's just that I'm looking at a problem or a new situation as if it is first grade and I'm a kindergartner.

Years later I ask my mother, "Do you remember the test we had to take in kindergarten?"

"Yes," she says.

"Did I do ok?"

"You were the top one in the class."

1943 - we move from New Britain to Plainville halfway through my kindergarten year. Judy is not in school yet and Tommy is only two, so I'm the only one in this new school and I have to make friends with a whole new roomful of kids.

The first day of school is foreign to me. The other kids know where the restrooms are and they all have blankets and cubbies to put them in when we are not lying down to take a rest. They all get milk in little cartons with straws. At the end of the morning I wait for my mother to come and get me. I don't yet know my way home.

I stand at the huge floor-to-ceiling windows and watch for her. A boy is waiting, too, and here comes his mother to pick him up! Where's *my* mother?

The teacher has waited with us, and now she has to leave. I am in the empty kindergarten room. The entire school seems empty, and *I don't know the way home!*

I hold myself together until I spot her pushing the baby carriage with Tommy in it. I rush out and grab her, pushing my face into her dress and sobbing with relief.

"What's the matter with you?" she demands, yanking me by the wrist. "I told you I would come get you!"

I'm so relieved that I never think to do what another child would do: stamp my foot and pout and say, "You *promised!*" Instead, I memorize my route that very day, so that this will not happen to me again.

✫ ✫ ✫

I am not allowed to wear blue. "Blue is Judy's color and green is yours, Barbara."

Check out my house and my clothes now—blue. Blue. Blue. I own one green shirt and I keep it just for St. Patrick's Day. I don't know if Judy wears green now.

My mother believes in One To A Customer, so she has decided that I will be the one learning to play the piano and Judy will be the one to go to art lessons. I don't know how she figured this one out, but it must have been a strong message, because to this day Judy only plays a little bit of piano and I draw like a fourth-grader.

Judy *has* artistic talent. She finds some old worn high heels that our mother threw out and she paints a picture of them. She wins a statewide award for this in high school. Our family drives to Hartford to see all the prizewinners from the high schools around Connecticut. My mother's embarrassed reaction: "Now people will know what kind of shoes I throw out into the trash."

Another shoe story: our high school colors are blue and white and I have a pair of blue heels that I am fond of. I am Valedictorian and after I give the graduation speech my parents come up to me. My Dad congratulates me—*all the awards you won, Barbara! And full tuition to Boston University* – and my mother says, "You were the only one there with blue shoes. What must people think?"

Judy has a wooden artist's box. We share a bedroom and when she isn't around I open it just to smell the oil colors and the turpentine. What a holy mystery this is to me, this art! When she is in fifth grade she creates a papier-mache giraffe that she puts carelessly up on a shelf in our little closet. Oh, she should set it on the dining room table at a place of honor, it is so *good*! It is of variegated jungle colors and lacquered and I love to run my hands over it, it has such satisfying dimensions to it. To this day I am still drawn to art that I can touch.

1949 - I am twelve and in sixth grade. I am a competitive snob about getting better grades than anyone else, and as a result I am great at taking tests without fully capturing and understanding the subject matter. I'm a champion speller.

At the Church of Our Savior (Episcopal) as it says on the sign in front, I am in the choir. Now I may not have artistic ability, but I can sing, and I can sing loud! I love reading music and my piano lessons have helped me here. One day my teacher even said to me, "Barbara, don't sing, so I can hear the other children." Singing alto is my forte.

Miss Hird, our ancient (to me) organist, needs time off, and I am asked to play as a substitute. I've never touched an organ, but I remember first grade and being a kindergartner and something is pushing at me to give this a try.

I won't have the nerve to touch the foot pedals for a year. The congregation is enthusiastically supportive. I have no memory of what I sound like, but they brave it through with me until Miss Hird comes back.

1955 - At Boston University, where I am enrolled in the School of Liberal Arts on a full-tuition ($600 a semester then) scholarship, I am asked the play the powerful Cassavant pipe organ in the chapel. For morning worship services. At seven o'clock in the morning.

I say yes. There's one catch: *since I am not in the School of Music, I am not allowed to practice.*

I cannot put my hands on the manuals or try out the various stops. So every weekday morning I sit at this impressive, intimidating pipe organ, my brow sweaty as I study the row after row of stops in front of me—it's a little like flying a plane without ever having been allowed to learn what the various toggles and levers are for—and I pull some on and pray that the music will be—not awful.

At our dorm, which houses 24 girls who do our own cooking and cleaning in this five-story Brownstone mansion, Harriet Richards House, we have erstwhile musicians from the School of Music, enough of them that a rule has been set up for the piano in the great room: if you play the same measure more than once, this is construed as practicing—and there is to be no practicing.

I'm glad, because we would be hearing scales all day long, and it is here that I learn to really play, since I can't go over a measure twice. It's also where I discover that I have as much musical talent as the girls in the Music program, and *why* didn't I get this choice when I applied for college?

This is why: my mother, who had never been to college, told Judy and me, "You girls can be teachers or nurses or secretaries or housewives. That's it. Take your pick."

Years later when I went back to college I taught piano as a way to pay for my tuition. So I guess she was right—I became a teacher.

632 Arch Street, New Britain, Connecticut | 19

**Brother Tom, Friend Judy Bailey, Sister Judy, me,
Friend Sally Tolli, her sister Nancy.
About 1948.**

There is a Tavern in the Town

If you look at my hometown of Plainville, Connecticut from my old house, the main streets make a rough "Y". You cut across the Bailey's back yard (often enough that the grass won't grow there), past the trash heap with discarded bottles of formaldehyde from the funeral home— and on lucky days, discarded fresh funeral flowers to bring home and stick in a milk bottle vase—; in front of Bailey's you could walk across the street to where Sally Tolli, my oldest friend and my "second family" live; or just stay on this side of the street and go 20 steps to the corner where Rizzo's market is, and the traffic light, where Smokey the Policeman makes sure we cross safely.

If you went to the left you would reach Broad Street school on the other side of the train tracks. You would have to be careful and not put a penny on the track or a train would come by and fall over. You would also have to be careful and hold your breath when you passed the Catholic Church on the way to school or someone could rush out and grab you and make you a Catholic.

I didn't make any of that up. Older, wiser school kids told me this.

But we're not going left today; we're following the trunk of the "Y" from Rizzo's up Whiting Street to the center of town, past the fire station and the post office where they list photos of the 10 Most Wanted Men and the rewards we kids will receive when we spot one of those bad guys hanging around in Plainville. Then past the fish market with its smells and Rogers Bakery with much better smells and the 5 and 10 and we're at the fork of the "Y".

Take the right fork and we're at the library where I received one of my most treasured gifts in my life—my own library card. (Mrs. Tolli took me to get it—I was too timid.) If we go six miles more that way we will be in New Britain. That's where I have my piano lessons and I'm only nine years old, getting on a bus by myself and then walking for blocks to my lesson in the basement of a music store.

I have a ritual on my way to the lesson—I stop at the 5 & 10 there, which boasts a doughnut-making machine. The oil has probably never been changed, and I never have the money to buy a doughnut, but I love to watch the nozzle squirt out dough and plop it into the oil, where it moves through the melted browning grease until a paddle turns it over. It's mechanical and wonderful.

I love my male music teacher, who looks like Wendell Corey, the movie star, but I don't love him enough to practice until the morning of my lesson. One day he tells me he is leaving.

My heart breaks. "Where are you going?" I ask, trying not to cry. "What will I tell my mother?"

"Tell her—I'm going to China," he laughs.

When I report this to her she narrows her eyes and snorts.

I can't afford to buy the sheet music that's on the racks in the music store, so I read hungrily through it, memorizing as much as I can, and then practice it from my head when I get home. Today I can play almost any popular song you want to sing, without first seeing the music.

As long as it's before 1980.

If we take the left fork in the center of town we will cross the railroad tracks and there will be the Strand movie theater on our right. I develop a discerning passion there for films. It has never left me.

Ahead several blocks will be the Episcopal Church of Our Savior, where we kids go to Sunday School and I will, at age 12, be talked into playing the organ for services, even though I've never yet had an organ lesson. If we go to the next town we will be in Bristol, the future home of ESPN Sports Network.

Across the street from the movies (14 cents for kids unless you have to confess that you have turned 13) is a tavern with odd smells coming from it. A side door reads "Ladies Entrance".

I muse to myself about this: why do ladies need their own door? Does it go to a different room in the tavern? I've never, of course, been inside a tavern, but I can picture ladies going in there with hats and gloves on, sitting in their own room and sipping tea. As far as I can tell, there are no windows on this tavern, except one in front; so there would have to be pretty pictures on the walls to make up for this lack.

My grandmother Alo has warned me *never* to walk down the street while smoking a cigarette and holding a leash with a dog at the end of it. (I never have.) So—are *these* not ladies? And does this mean that they could go in by the front door? And if so, are they allowed to bring their dogs with them?

I sense that I would get only a vague answer if I ask, so I keep these questions to myself.

There's a bigger one for me: I see scruffy men hanging around the tavern. I have plenty of time to study them while standing in line for the afternoon movie with a bunch of noisy school friends. These men have an unwashed, unshaven appearance. They look as though they don't brush their teeth or their hair.

And I never see women hanging around on the streets. There have to be lone women, but where are they? All the women I ever see are clean and neat; so I figure that when women get old, they can always live with a family and do dishes or wash clothes or cook for them, which means that from birth to death there's always a job for a woman to do, and this makes me very glad I am a female woman.

But men? Men are an unknown species. They go, I guess, like my Dad, to work in the morning and disappear from our lives, and then return home for supper. Or like Mr. Bailey, they go into the basement of the funeral home and work. But these men at the tavern look as though they don't have a wife or a mother or children and I feel very sorry for them.

(There's another man I feel sorry for. He's an underweight middle-aged black man. I see him in the post office from time to time. He puts white makeup on his face, which runs down his face in streaks, and I want to say to him, "Don't do that! Be proud of being the color you are!")

But I'm just a kid, so I don't. But I don't laugh at him, either, the way some of the boys in my class do.

I bring my younger sister Judy and younger brother Tommy to the movies. Each ticket is 14 cents— times three equals 42 cents with eight cents left over, just enough for candy. We argue in front of the candy counter. I want Necco Wafers. There are a lot of them to a pack and they last pretty long. I like the licorice-flavored ones.

The inside is dark and cool, as I remember, even before the days of air conditioning. We find seats. The place is alive with children, talking, yelling, clapping for the movie to start. I have to be A Good Example for my sister and brother, so I sit quietly, reading the green letters "E X I T" over and over in my head.

There's always the quandary of Tommy and the bathroom. I make sure he visits the bathroom before we leave home, but as soon as we get inside the theater he starts dancing up and down. He insists on the men's room, but I'm not supposed to leave him alone, so I usually take him, protesting like mad, into the ladies' room.

"Next time go at home," both Judy and I tell him.

"I did! I did! I don't want to go where the *girls* are!" He pulls at my hand and threatens to give me an Indian rope burn, but I'm older and stronger than he is.

Two o'clock and the movies begin! First there's a cartoon—my favorite is Bugs Bunny because nothing ever gets the better of him. Sometimes there's a second cartoon and one miraculous Saturday there were *twelve* cartoons in a row! We all cheered in disbelief as the next one came on, and then the next one!

Then there are previews of coming attractions and then a newsreel. After that comes a shorter film—Roy Rogers or Hopalong Cassidy. They always end their movies sitting and laughing. When they laugh you know it's the end of the movie.

Then the main movie comes on, and after that, the whole thing starts over again, so that you can stay in the theater from afternoon until night and never have to pay for another ticket or get up and leave. Once Judy and I did that and we got home about nine o'clock at night, forgetting about supper.

We'd come home from Western movies whinnying like horses and we'd gallop around the house until Dad told us to go outside, because we sounded like sick cows.

I thought Dad looked like Randolph Scott.

There was always a fight scene in a Western, in a saloon. There was always a fistfight at the top of the stairs and two men would topple over the wooden railing and come crashing down onto a poker table. I never liked that—I wondered who would clean up afterward and I figured it would have to be *me*.

It was an odd juxtaposition, a tavern and a movie theater across the street from each other.

✯ ✯ ✯

November, 1963: my husband has been out of town on a business trip and I decide to buy him a bottle of southern Comfort—his favorite—for his return.

I drive to the liquor store near the beach. I've never been in it before and I'm not sure I've ever been in *any* kind of liquor store in my life, thanks to my grandmother's warnings. It's afternoon and sunny. No scruffy men hang around outside, I am relieved to see.

There is one man inside the store and he is talking to the owner. Deep in conversation, they both glance up and then ignore me.

A radio on the counter is on and there seems to be some kind of pandemonium coming from it. The two men in the store keep talking and I lean in toward the radio to listen. I say to the men, "Something's happening!" The owner looks at me, frowns at the radio, and turns up the volume.

That's where I am when I hear that President Kennedy has been assassinated.

It is ten years before I venture inside a liquor store again.

Ruth Carlson Rackliffe.

Tales from Behind the Funeral Home

4th of July, 2013:

I'm listening to the distant boom-boom of firecrackers. My cat has hidden under a tent I've made for her from her favorite blanket. Her baleful stare lets me know this all my fault. The sound of fireworks takes me right back to my childhood.

When I was young, in Plainville, Connecticut (pop. 10,000, town established 1869), we four children (my youngest sister Alice wouldn't be born until I was an embarrassed 13), mother, father, and grandparents, moved to a little two story 100-year-old house with a packed-earth floor cellar and one bathroom, right behind the town's only funeral home.

My parents had no idea what a rich childhood we were about to have.

The Bailey Funeral Home had been in the family for several generations, and the Bailey grandchildren were the same ages as us Rackliffe kids.

Their father was a flamboyant person. If he'd lived to be 90 he might have become the town "character". They owned a pony named Pickles (which once kicked me in the knee), a bevy of monkeys (more later), an old-fashioned sleigh to come pick us up after school on snowy days, with me waving a mittened hand like a dowager queen at my envious friends and pretending I was a princess, and a German Shepherd named Lady. And a mother who was the first one in town to get a short curly permanent wave, who owned a mink coat, a tiger-print two-piece strapless Bikini and a Cadillac convertible. Oh, my parents looked so dull by comparison!

And how about the iron Civil War cannon that Mr. Bailey planted in his back yard right next to ours!

How did he come about getting this cannon from the center of town? We had no idea, nor did we think about it. It was just another toy for us. It was *huge*, enormously heavy, a kind of worn greenish-gray color—and if enough of us climbed on the muzzle, would tilt down to the ground suddenly—*BOOMP!*—, making us all shriek with surprise as the ground shook. Then we'd climb to the other end and tilt it upwards again.

Nobody ever came out to tell us, "Stop that right *now*! You're going to get killed!" If any mother yelled at us I've forgotten about it. This was too much fun.

And who else had *ever* had a Civil War cannon in the backyard adjoining ours?

The 4th of July was a day we girls knew to dread—this was the day when boys lit their cherry bombs and tiny Chinese firecrackers and threw these explosive poppers at our feet, making us run away screaming while they laughed like mad at us. It was a day of male burned fingers and hands and the smell of something different, yet compelling, in the air.

Then the finale! Mr. Bailey strode over to the cannon to make a homemade bomb. We followed like faithful soldiers, yelling, "He's gonna make a bomb!" He poured gunpowder into the long muzzle and then wadded newspaper into it. He warned us all to stay back (and we were scared enough of his temper to do so).

He tamped down the inside the muzzle of the cannon and lit a rope fuse. We kids waited, our eyes wide, our hands to our ears, glancing at each other to see if anyone would get scared and run away.

PHOOMP! A deafening sound, a huge puff of smoke, a shudder from the cannon. Where did the charge go? Did it hit another house, set a yard on fire? We didn't know or care. All we knew was that excitement followed this man, and we all wanted to follow that excitement.

At a safe distance.

Aluminum and Wrought Iron

See this pie pan? It belonged to my grandmother Alice Elizabeth Hart Rackliffe. It's aluminum, ten inches in diameter. It reads "Aladdin Universal Aluminum" on the back. There are numbers there too, but time has rubbed them away like names on an ancient gravestone. It's more than a hundred years old.

So many pies have been baked in this pan that the knife cuts look like a multitudinous array emanating from a central sun, impossible to count. When I am gone, one of my children will inherit it and someone will most likely throw it away—and why not? It's a nondescript pie pan. They never knew my grandmother, except through what traits I have inherited from her.

I'm the only one now who remembers standing at the kitchen table, resting my chin on its cold porcelain surface, watching my grandmother create cherry and apple pies with so-flaky crusts made of lard.

She never measured anything. I watched in awe as she peeled apples, the skin falling away in one long curly piece. If we kids were lucky, she gave us each a tiny leftover dab of the pie dough and we'd roll them out into dingy gray rounds from our never-totally clean hands. Then we'd sprinkle our dough with cinnamon and sugar, to be baked along with hers, waiting while jiggling from one foot to the other, while eating little shards of apple.

Over the years the aluminum pie pan became encrusted with boiled-over sugar until there was a permanent bumpy hard black edge around the outside of the lip. I'd look at it and run my fingers over it and feel the love she'd put into those pies.

Once I dated a man who had a grown son nicknamed "Jake the Snake". Jake, wanting to do something nice for me since I'd brought him and his dad a homemade pie, shoved the pan into the oven and set the oven on "self-clean". The next day he presented me proudly with—a plain aluminum pan, the crust burned off.

Stunned, I looked at Jake's happy face and somehow kept myself from crying. This could have been *any* old pie pan now! Why couldn't he have realized its history?

Well, of course he couldn't. And I couldn't tell him about my grandmother, a Hart descendant of the Harts who founded Hartford, who once, when I asked her if our ancestors came over on the Mayflower, responded, "No—we waited 20 years and then came over on our *own* boat." She laughed when she said it, and yet years later I found on a map a "Rackliffe Island" off the coast of Maine. Could they have landed there? In their own boat? I liked her story better than any truth I might have discovered.

My Grandmother Alice, whom we called "Alo" at her request, had long gray hair that she knotted into a bun and then held in place with hair pins. She had a blue brimmed straw hat and when she went out once a week (probably to visit her sisters in New Britain), I would watch, scared and excited, as she drove a hatpin through her hair into that hat to keep it on. She never once skewered her head, and I couldn't figure out how she kept from suddenly jumping in pain. I was sure the pin would go right into her scalp.

She knew I had a passionate wish—to have curly hair. Mine was stick-straight and fine and in my school photos I looked like a refugee.

"Barbara," she told me, "if you eat your bread crusts it will give you curly hair."

Honestly? So I ate all of my toast, crust and all, for years, sure that I would have curly hair from this.

What I found out as an adult was that if I went to a beauty parlor and paid a bunch of money, I could have curly hair.

I never blamed her for this. I was a very skinny child and this was her way of fattening me up.

But to this day I leave a piece of crust on my plate when I eat toast. "That's for *you*, Alo," I think

My grandparents Rackliffe lived with us from the time I was an infant, so I never could remember a time without them. My first vivid memory was of sitting on the floor while two enormous pairs of legs loomed over me—my mother's and grandmother's—as I successfully tied my shoes. The sunshine bounced off the linoleum floor, so bright it hurt my eyes, and I recall total joy in doing something for myself with no help.

My grandfather Thomas Winship Rackliffe was blind. His pupils were opaque and I didn't like to look at them. I figured I would also go blind when I got old, since that seemed to be something that happened in our family—so I practiced playing the piano with my eyes shut, determined that I would know how to do something when I grew old and blind.

There were at least four different stories that relatives told me about how he had gone blind—he'd bumped into something; something had bumped into **him;** he had glaucoma; he had cataracts....

Whatever **had** happened, he sat in a Morris rocking chair beside the big wooden radio that I was sure held a miniature orchestra inside. It was my job to make sure he didn't accidentally rock on my younger brother Tom or baby brother John as he crawled about on the floor under Grandpa's feet.

The rocking chair had a lion head at the end of each wooden arm and I could sit and rest my hands on lions' heads when my grandfather took a nap in his bedroom. I would run my fingers into a groove by each head. My Dad had told me that when he was a boy he carved those grooves into the chair with his penknife. Since he was red-headed with loads of freckles, I could picture him doing that. Knowing my grandmother and her stern sense of right and wrong, he would have been punished—but he never told me that part.

(I lost track of the chair, rediscovering it decades later at my nephew's home. He'd recovered and refinished it and I sank into it, running my hands, larger now, over the lions' heads.

There were no grooves! My dad's handiwork was gone. "There were some funny holes there, so I filled them in," my nephew said proudly. Again I kept silent. Things pass, things pass. The memories sustain us.)

Once a week, as I said, my grandmother pinned her hat to her head and got ready to leave.

"Where are you going, Alo?" I would ask, wanting to go, too.

"I"m going to pack my bags and go to Boston," she would say.

Or, "I"m going to see a man about a horse."

A horse! Then I *really* wanted to go with her.

She taught me by example that caregivers needed to take time off. She took such loving care of my grandfather—he must have had trouble with his teeth, because she made him a lot of toast—crusts and all— with warm milk on it—but she also had a life away from him.

She had a treadle sewing machine. If we got down on the floor we could make the treadle go up and down by pushing it with our hands. The treadle was black metal and had some kind of open-weave pattern with the letters "S-I-N-G-E-R" stamped into it.

She sewed clown costumes for my younger sister Judy and me one Halloween. I was probably six and Judy was five. The costumes had buttons down the fronts and ruffles around the cuffs and the neck. Mine was blue and white polka dots and Judy's was a red and green print. This put me into consternation: I couldn't decide if I envied Judy's costume or liked mine better. I wanted them *both*, even though I knew I couldn't wear both of them at once.

So many questions I should have asked my grandparents back then! But I was a child and thought that life went on forever.

There's a fourth grade photo of my class, taken a month after my grandmother died and six months after my grandfather's death. In the photo I look as shell-shocked as if I have been hit by a wrecking ball. I was not yet nine.

The next year, in fifth grade, I seem to have recovered. If you looked at the two photos, you would not think that was the same girl.

For years I had dreams that I was pushing back against a wrought-iron fence and sobbing as though my heart would break. Twenty years ago I went back to New Britain and to St. Mark's Episcopal Church, where my family had gone until we had moved to Plainville halfway through my kindergarten year.

I asked someone in the church office if she could possibly find my grandparents' records. Inside of five minutes I was staring at an old oversized Church Records book with "1945-1946" stamped on the cover. And *there* were my grandparent's names and dates of death, as well as causes of death—heart disease for my grandfather and cancer for my grandmother. I was seeing for the first time what they had died from.

It took a while to find the old cemetery where the records said they were buried, the city had changed so since I was there last. Once there, I asked a custodian where I might find the Rackliffe graves and there they were!—so many of them, going back almost two hundred years! I walked around, taking photos, studying the gravestone dates—then I looked up. Not eight feet from my grandmother's grave was a wrought iron fence.

I pictured a thin little left-handed girl, with brown eyes and straight brown hair held in place by a plastic barrette, unnoticed by her family, trying not to fall apart, not to be a bother to them—and I said to her, "It's okay. It's okay. We made it."

I never again had the wrought iron fence dream.

Going-Going-Gone!

Our family did not show their emotions in front of us, even when our grandparents died), except sometimes for my mother, who, despite her Swedish blood, would have a couple of highballs when the relatives got together at our house, and then would play the piano boldly, smoke Camel after Camel, and try to flirt with Uncle Howard, Dad's youngest brother, who was a talented painter and undoubtedly was gay.

"Your mother is an enigma, Varvara," he told me once, using the Russian name (I guessed) for "Barbara". He also raised Russian Wolfhounds, which from time to time he fed while the dogs stood on top of our kitchen table when my mother was not around. (This was after my grandmother had died or Alo would have "given him what for".)

He also spent a lot of time in our one bathroom when he dropped in for one of his surprise, lengthy visits. He smoked Turkish cigarettes and abhorred ashtrays. We could count the length of his stays by the number of charred cigarette spots in the bathroom windowsill beside the toilet. We kids spent our time hopping on one leg and pounding on the door, "I gotta go! I gotta go, Howard!"

Howard was immune to our needs. (My brothers could make a dash if nobody noticed, to the lilac bush at the far edge of our yard. Judy and I were not so lucky.)

But this story is not yet about Howard. It's about my mother and how her assigning of chores led to my first big furniture buy.

We were all aware that Tommy, three years younger than me, two years younger than my sister Judy, and a *boy*, was Mom's favorite. One can only imagine the disappointment she felt on having two daughters in a row first. I never understood this, especially after my three daughters came first and were such treats.

Tommy was given the easiest chore in the house and he balked at even this.

"Take out the trash by the back door, Tommy," I would tell him. He would scowl—I don't have to listen to you, his look would tell me. "You're not the boss of me," would be his answer, and it was so true.

He would disappear into the backyard of the Bailey's house and Mom would make me take out the trash in his place, since she couldn't find him and trash was mounting in front of the door to our back stoop where we hung the wash on the clothesline.

"Barbara, you take the trash out, " Mom would sigh—where *was* that boy?— and order me.

"But it's *Tommy's* job—!"

"Just take it out. How will people get by?"

Oh, how the unfairness of it all rankled.

On top of that, Judy and I were given the chore of doing the evening dishes. The sink was in an alcove off the kitchen—in better homes it might have been a butler's pantry, I dreamed—and it faced a blank wall. There was a window opposite the sink which looked onto the side porch—but what good was a window like that? Nobody could look out of it unless they climbed onto the lid of our old green Easy washing machine with rollers that once had caught Judy's arm.

I yearned for a window.

One summer day when I was ten I headed to the town center, a five-minute walk away from home. This day, as on all others, I walked slowly, my head down, looking for any loose change that someone might have dropped. I never found any, but that didn't make me give up my search.

And this day was different! Today I had a *quarter* that a relative had given me! I held it clutched in my fist in my pocket—I wasn't going to drop this precious coin so somebody else, eyes looking down at the sidewalk, could pick it up before I could notice it was gone! My hand was sweaty, but I kept it in my pocket.

I was musing about how I always looked down and Judy always looked up—so much so that she kept tripping on the edges of the sidewalks and I had to grab her before she fell down. Sometimes I think that this was what made Judy as an adult a very talented painter of landscapes and not of concrete.

I heard an unfamiliar commotion at an old house near Rogers' Bakery. I crossed the street and headed for the sound, which was coming from the backyard. Folding metal chairs had been set up. There were furniture, dishes, glassware and other items on the grass. It looked as though the house had exploded its contents onto the backyard lawn. I'd never seen anything like this before.

A burly man stood in front of the furniture. He was calling out numbers and the dozen or so people in the folding chairs were answering him back.

This was my first auction and to me it was like being dropped onto an alien planet. I soaked up the sights and sounds and, as only young children can, imagined myself invisible in the crowd.

I probably was. People didn't pay much attention to children in those days unless the children got into trouble. Then grownups yelled and they didn't bother to figure out whose child it was. That child just needed yelling at.

I stood at the back. Maybe all those people *owned* those chairs and would get mad at me if I sat in one! I watched carefully to see what the rules of this new game were.

Ah—the oversized man put his hand on something and gave a number—"Let's start this at one dollar, folks," he called. Then someone said, "One dollar," and someone else said, "Two," and the one who said the most money when the man stopped them got the prize.

This was fascinating to me, this new look into Big People world. I watched, my quarter in my fist.

Then I saw it! It was a big heavy wooden mantel from a dining room buffet. It stood on end, off by itself. There was no buffet to go with it. It had a glass mirror that ran its length. The mirror had some flyspecks on it, but it wasn't cracked. There was a narrow shelf beneath the glass—the perfect place to set a soap dish! I measured it with my eye—it looked just the right length to go over our kitchen sink.

The large man moved to the mantel. "How much for this piece?" he said. "Real mahogany."

My hand shot up. "Twenty-five cents!" I said, my voice dry.

The man looked over at me. "How much, young lady?" he smiled.

"Twenty-five cents!" I said, aware of people's stares, and with a stronger voice now.

There was some laughter and then a slim young woman in a hat raised her hand and said, "One dollar!"

Everyone looked back at me. I shook my head. "I just have a quarter," I said.

"I said one dollar!" the woman repeated more firmly. The burly man hesitated.

Suddenly a man at my side said, "Let the little girl have it!"

The crowd yelled, "Yes! Let her have it!"

The man in charge pounded his open hand on the mantle. "Sold!" he called out. "Twenty-five cents!"

"But—but—" protested the woman," I was going to put plants on it—!"

Nobody listened. The people were, for some reason, applauding me. The man in front put out his hand and I dropped my sweaty quarter into his palm. "How will you get it home?" he asked.

This hadn't occurred to me.

"I'll drive it to her house," one of the men near me volunteered. "I have a truck."

My brother Tommy was impressed—somebody's truck in front of our house and his sister in the front seat! My mother fussed around, straightening magazines and apologizing for the look of the place to a stranger who brought the mantel inside and even helped my Dad bolt it to the wall, where it fit—perfectly. I could hear him telling Dad about how I had bid for the mirrored piece.

"I am half sick of shadows," said the Lady of Shalotte, who in the poem could only see life by looking into a mirror at its reflection.

I now felt like that Lady, my hands in gray soapy Ivory dishwater, my eyes looking into the mirror which now reflected the window behind me and brought me the outside.

I have been passionate about auctions ever since. And I'm always on the lookout for some child who might have just a quarter to bid.

And about Tommy's job taking out the trash? Along with the "curly hair" bread crust piece of my past, which I recognize full well, is my leaving a trash basket by the door to the garage for a bit before I take it outside to the recycle barrel.

Take that, Tommy.

✶ ✶ ✶

My brother Johnny, grandmother Alice Rackliffe (Alo) and brother Tommy.

Howard Rackliffe.

The Painter of Mustard and Ketchup

Our Uncle Howard Eugene Rackliffe was Dad's youngest brother of four boys. He never married—his overriding passion in life was painting.

"Your grandmother wanted a girl, you know," whispered one of my aunts to me one day when I was young. "You see his initials—H.E.R.? *HER*, that's what—for a *girl*."

She was confiding in the wrong person. As my grandmother's first granddaughter, I enjoyed some special attention from Alo, and I wasn't about to give that up.

Howard never had a permanent home. He traveled from friend to friend with a few clothes and his oils. He never stayed too long at our house—there were too many noisy kids here, and he loved to sleep late and then bang out songs of his own creation with crashing discordant chords on the piano before mixing himself a weird breakfast of whatever he could find in the refrigerator, dumping it all into the frying pan—eggs, pickles, leftover gravy, beets—and then leaving the crusted pan for Mom or me to clean.

He used the same refrigerator ingredients as paints. I was serious about the ketchup and the mustard. He was blindingly wedded to painting—I doubt there was any other world for him.

He also had tight curly hair, which I envied. "Did you eat your bread crusts when you were little, Howard?" I asked, not expecting and not getting a reply. He was busy finding just the right shade of yellow to paint a picture of my teddy bear.

He loved Maine and painted many landscapes and seascapes of the rugged land—nothing like a Norman Rockwell—all in his own modernistic style.

Once he had a retrospective of his paintings in the gallery at the Aetna building in Hartford. I entered the enormous room and my mouth dropped open. Here were hundreds and hundreds of paintings, done by a man who had a world in his head that he needed to get onto canvas as fast as he could.

Howard waited for me to leave. "What did you think, Varvara?" he asked gently.

I couldn't talk. The immensity of his luminescent work had brought tears into my eyes and throat.

His paintings are in some fine galleries in New England. I own three of them myself, proudly. I had two more, large as doors, and I lent them to son Jon, whose new wife went into a rage one day and destroyed them with a screwdriver, chopping away at them like the character in the "Psycho" shower scene.

Jon was in veterinary school at the time and was heartbroken. I phoned an art gallery in Maine and was told that each painting was valued at a little over $8000 each. The wife of six weeks agreed to a divorce without making Jon pay alimony.

Thank you for keeping Jon safe, Howard. I still have the pieces and maybe someday I'll frame them and give family members each a bit of their great-uncle's work.

Howard was in Hartford at one time and he went into a restaurant where a dozen of his paintings hung. An indignant hostess turned him away, thinking him to be a panhandler, although his old clothes were clean and so was his curly beard. He didn't protest. The owner went running down the street after him to bring him back.

Dad told me that when Howard was in the hospital in Hartford, dying from his erratic nutritional lifestyle and Turkish cigarettes, that Howard's friends lined the corridors there.

"He was living in a tiny apartment, Barb," Dad phoned me. "After he died I went and got some valuables of his out of there—a fan, some books and phonograph records—"

"His paintings, Dad," I urged, feeling so helplessly far away in Florida. *"Did you get his paintings?"*

"Oh, those, " said my 86-year-old Dad, showing that he was still Howard's oldest brother, the kind caretaker of all of us family members, even if he didn't quite understand artistic temperament. "No, I didn't. I'll go back there and get them in a couple of weeks."

Me, one month after my grandmother's death – fourth grade.

Ya Load Sixteen Tons and Here's What Ya Get

When I was in junior high school my mother found me a summer job ironing clothes for a very large woman who had trouble breathing. I figured it was from some ailment until I saw how she spent her days eating from five-pound boxes of chocolates, none of which she ever offered me.

This woman wanted me to iron *everything*. I ironed socks. I pressed washcloths and towels. She drew the line at nylons, fortunately. Now, I knew how to iron clothes. I'd been doing this since I was nine. But I had never ironed socks.

Late every afternoon her husband would come home and bring her some more candy.

"Look at my precious wife," he would beam, pointing her out to me, as though she hadn't just spent the afternoon watching me iron and complaining about the weather and her life in general, "Isn't she just wonderful?"

The Wonderful Woman would sigh and wave a hand at him, as though this was even more effort than she could maintain. "He knows how hard I work," she would say to me.

But at least I was out of the rain.

When I was a year older, I was given a job as Senior counselor for a Girl Scout Day Camp. This consisted of digging latrines, watching the girls while they swam in a manmade pond, and building campfires. There were two of us counselors and 18 Girl Scouts, just a little younger than us.

The other counselor had long light blonde hair. Mine was short and straight. The theme for the Day Camp was "Snow White". Guess who was immediately named "Snow White"? Guess who was then named "The Wicked Witch"?

As soon as those giggling girls named us they began treating us like our pseudonyms, cuddling up to Snow White and screaming in mock terror and running away from me.

It was a long four weeks. I earned a dollar a day.

So ironing and digging ditches were not to be my callings. As a favor, a high school friend got me a job phoning everyone in the telephone book, A to Z, and trying to convince them, in July, to buy storm windows. This kid pictured himself as an entrepreneur, apparently. He set me up in his aunt's house, in a room upstairs that had its own phone, and put me to work.

"Don't give them your real name, Barb," was the only training he gave me. So I was Miss Jones, and several more men tried to date me over the phone than tried to buy storm windows.

But since I was being paid on a "how many windows can I sell?" basis by my school friend, I decided one Saturday morning that I would put in some more time, so I walked to the aunt's house and let myself in through the unlocked front door. As I walked upstairs I had a feeling of something being not quite right about this job— it was the snoring that tipped me off: the aunt and her family were still sound asleep.

There was no way I could sell windows in that private an atmosphere— I was so sure I would be arrested for trespassing and would the kid who hired me back *me* up or his aunt?— so I tiptoed downstairs and outside again, shutting the front door as quietly as I could and then running away. I never went back. Miss Jones had made her last phone call for the storm windows people

In the summer between my junior and senior years I found a job within walking distance of our house. It involved machinery and magnifying glasses.

You've seen big springs with the end loop of the springs bent into a 90 degree angle from the rest of the spring. Picture a metal coil. Now bend one end and/or the other halfway out. Now give its creator a name—Loop Bender.

Now make those springs ve-r-r-y tiny, so that in order to bend them you have to look through a magnifying glass. Under the glass you take the spring, secure it on a metal bed beneath a sharp sort of cleaver, and with your foot press so the the cleaver comes down fast—bang!—and bends the end coil.

Now do that many many many times a day. *That* was my job.

The job wasn't hard. It was tedious, but not anything that strained my brain.

No, the hardest parts of the job were the bathroom and the doughnut truck.

The doughnut truck came by in the middle of the morning and the eight of us working in this small one-room shop would take a break and go out to the truck to buy a snack.

I loved glazed doughnuts, especially since I didn't know how they were made. They tasted fresh enough and not as though they had come from the 5 & 10 of my youth. I also got used to drinking black coffee.

But all that sugar was binding to my insides and all the coffee was diuretic. And the only bathroom in the workroom was a made-over closet in the center of the room, with no window. I discovered on my first day of work that whenever anyone used the bathroom, all conversation ceased, and then the person who emerged from that room was subjected to a slew of bathroom odor humor jokes.

I was not to be a victim of that, so I held myself together every day until I could get home at noon. I worried daily about what would happen if I ever got a job farther away from home than I could walk.

The workers, men and women of indistinct ages, did a lot of jokes about s-e-x. They would look at me, the youngest (and certainly most virginal) of the group, check to see if I understood what they were talking about, and then make another euphemism-laden joke about how each one was doing at home or at a bar or in the back seat of a car.

"Oh, she got—you know—last night. Right, Sheila? Don't Dottie look just like she got—you know—"(a nod in my direction)"—last night?"

"Yeah," someone else would chime in, "how's your *husband* after all that— you know— last night, Dottie? Can he even *walk* today?" A round of blustery laughter at this.

Raw jokes abounded. I don't remember any of them.

But I was busy! I was being paid in piecework terms! Piecework meant being paid by the piece, or in our cases, since the springs were so small, by the ounce. Wow! The faster I worked, the more money I could make!

In two weeks I had broken all records. Since I had made no friends with the other workers, I neglected to pay attention to their grumbling about me.

In two weeks I had broken all previous records. In two weeks and one day I was fired.

I had learned valuable lessons, like: piecework doesn't mean what it says it means; always look for a place of business that has nice bathrooms with windows; and if everyone could tell by looking at faces the day after, who had sex and who didn't, we'd all be wearing stories on our countenances.

The summer was half over and I was fired. I was trying to save money for college and I was jobless. Fortunately someone from our church found me a job for the rest of the summer in steel strapping.

Of course you know what steel strapping is, unless sixty years after I had my job, they don't make it any more. I worked at Stanley Works in New Britain and unless you've been cloistered, you know what Stanley Tools are.

Steel strapping goes around heavy boxes and wooden crates like belts and then a heavy-duty snap holds the ends together. You have to use a metal-cutting tool to get the strapping loose.

My job was to file orders away. I went at it with fervor, determined to find mistakes in filing. Then my boss would say, *"Hooray for Barbara! She saved the day for us and kept us from making a costly wrong-filing error! Barbara is our hero!"*

I stopped looking after I found a couple of misfiled papers, showed them to my boss, and he said without looking up, " Okay. Just file them correctly."

It was there that I learned how to play cards at lunch. I learned from a Catholic girl working there that she could see any movie she wanted and then would go for absolution and the priest had to forgive her. I learned that if you were in the middle of an intersection and a firetruck came by, it could run your car over and you couldn't sue, couldn't get a penny, because a firetruck *always* has the right of way!

I learned something a man should never say to his wife: *"I told her, 'Honey, hurry up and get me to work, because it's air-conditioned and the house isn't.'* " That man faced a grim woman every evening when she picked him up at work. And I didn't blame her.

For a year after that job whenever I saw some steel strapping, I was as cheerfully proud of Stanley Works as if I'd poured the molten metal myself.

All the News that's Fit to Sit

After my grandparents died we could all fit in the kitchen, which is where we moved our suppertime. The dining room table was now for homework and Thanksgiving.

Alo had done most of the cooking—her roast beef and Yorkshire pudding and apple pies could not be duplicated— and, given my mother's somewhat terrified approach to cuisine, I was frankly scared of Mom's way of cooking.

To give my mother her due, with Alo at the stove there had been no place for Mom there. So when Mom started putting meals together with no grandmotherly backup, she did not have much confidence. She had been married for twelve years and had only boiled water and made Swedish coffee with eggshells.

Now she would peer into the oven and then straighten up, a worried look on her face.

"I think I'll call this done."

She thinks she'll call our food *"done"*? What could this mean? Could I trust her for my survival? Many years later I would see a movie about a dysfunctional family who refused to eat their sister's turkey because she had baked it in a slow oven overnight and they feared food poisoning.

That family made sense to me, even though her boyfriend bravely ate the turkey *and* the stuffing and didn't suffer any ill effects. I knew that was a movie and Mom's cooking was Real Life.

Now, my chair at the table was closest to the door to the cellar. On the other side of that door were steep wooden stairs leading to a hard packed dirt floor. The oil burner furnace was down there, and also stacks of jarred fruits and vegetables that my mother had put up. I refused to try them. Nothing edible could survive if it was sitting in that dank cellar!

I wouldn't even try the crab apple jelly my grandmother had cooked and put up, back when she was alive. I trusted my grandmother, but I had once bitten into a crab apple and it had so set my teeth on edge that I was positive the jelly tasted like that, too.

Eve would never have gotten in trouble if the snake had given her a crab apple to eat from the Tree of Knowledge. One bite was enough knowledge in that line for me.

None of us wanted to go into the cellar, so my mother stacked magazines and newspapers on the seat of my chair until one of us kids would volunteer to take them down.

None of us did, of course. The rule of childhood was to get out of doing as much work as possible until caught and yelled at. As a result, I kept growing higher and higher in my chair as I sat on a week's worth of the New Britain *Herald*.

I also read books at the table. I figured it this way: if the food was bad I wouldn't notice it while I was reading.

This was the time of day my mother could be sure to have my father's attention. My father might have been captive, but he was well-armed. He loved peanut butter, and he would slather it on celery. Between the crunching of the celery stalks and the mouth-gumming properties of the Peter Pan, he could get away with not answering her.

"Les," she would then say, turning her attention to me, "Barbara's reading a book at the table."

No reply from Dad. I would keep my eyes on the page. No reply from me, either. Judy, Tommy and Johnny would watch, eyes round, to see what would happen.

A long pause. Then, from Dad, a so-mild address, like the wing of a butterfly against a cheek: "Barbara, put your book down."

It hurt me to ignore him, but I did so.

"Les, you *have* to make her stop reading at the table—"

No reply, as we co-conspirators gummed the peanut butter or turned a page. I was safe until the next time

I rarely saw my mother sit with us. Oh, she had a chair, but stood instead, and if anyone finished a plate of food, piled some more on it over our protests. She hovered between the stove and the table, a nervous eye on us, ready to take any lack of appetite personally.

"Remember the starving children in Europe," she reminded us. "In *Europe!*"

She'd never been to Europe, so all of her information was from lengthy local phone conversations with her relatives. Her parents had come here from Sweden when they were three years old, so I didn't believe that counted.

"They can have my food," I would think to myself. Why in the world starving children would be drawn to my mother's supper plates I never dared ask. Even so, according to her, Starving Children in Europe were not to be trifled with. She could always play on our guilt so that we would eat more.

I knew that if I cleaned my plate she would add more to it. So I always left a little smidgen of potatoes or peas. That signaled to her that I was full. I do it to this day.

✲ ✲ ✲

When our five children were young I wanted no such fights over food at dinnertime, so I told them, "If you don't like what I'm serving, don't complain about it—just go get yourself a bowl of cereal and I won't be mad."

I remember one evening when they came to the kitchen for dinner, looked at what was on the table, and all five marched in silence to the cupboard for bowls and cereal boxes. I bit my tongue and kept my end of the bargain. To this day, the memory of their put-upon faces still makes me break out in a laugh.

✲ ✲ ✲

The Store on the Corner

There were no more apple pies after Alo died. Now we split for dessert a can of sugary/syrupy fruit cocktail, fruit pieces that none of us kids liked except for the cherry—and there was only one bit of cherry per can. We kids worked out some kind of gentlemen's agreement and told Dad he could have it. That was hard, because we all wanted it.

The store at the corner of Whiting and Broad Streets, a short walk away if we cut through the Bailey's yard (which we did), was owned by Mr. and Mrs. Rizzo. They had come here from Italy after the First World War. She was short and rather jolly, and he was reminiscent of a sad Abraham Lincoln with an Italian accent. The store smelled like garlic and onions and when I had any spare coins I would ask Mr. Rizzo to slice me some Swiss cheese. I don't know what vitamin or mineral I was deficient in, but the few slices of Swiss cheese filled my need. I never shared them with anyone.

In the winter there would be a half-dozen old Italian men sitting around the kerosene stove in the middle of the store, talking in Italian with arm-sweeping gestures and barely looking up when we kids came to buy a loaf of bread or a dozen eggs.

I interviewed Mrs. Rizzo once for a school project. I wish I still had the paper. She was fascinating to me and I got a look at a whole different world and time. When she talked about home in Italy she became quite animated and it was all I could do to write down her words and follow her accent at the same time

She was short and chubby and her husband was tall and gaunt. We owed money on our grocery bill always, as did many others. "Put it on the bill," we learned to say, and Mr. Rizzo would bring out a bunch of strips of butcher paper with an oversized metal clip at one end. He'd riffle through them and find the "Rackliffe" one. Then he'd wet the point of a pencil stub in his mouth and laboriously write down the total of what we'd just bought, along with the date.

Mr. Rizzo was the one who taught me how to carry numbers. He'd write a tiny number, the one to be carried, at the bottom of the numbers, so he could double-check his addition.

I still do that and I still remember Mr. Rizzo's taking the time to teach me. Why did he bother with me? I filched over the years probably a dozen Hershey Bars (my other food need). Kids are so transparent when they steal and I'm sure I was too, and yet he never reprimanded me. My guilty conscience and nothing else made me stop.

When my mother would give us $25, a quarter of my Dad's weekly paycheck, to take to Rizzo's market, we would try to give the dollar bills to *Mrs.* Rizzo, because she would become ecstatic and then she would say in an excited voice, "Go! Go! Pick-a yourself a pint-a ice cream!"

Then we'd peer into the big white metal ice chest where the ice cream and the Popsicles were stored, and argue over which kind to take home.

Six of us splitting a pint of ice cream: I don't know that I've ever enjoyed ice cream more. I trusted *that* food! And I remember it as a special time with family, eating ice cream.

✭ ✭ ✭

Mr. Rizzo went down into his store cellar one night, put a gun in his mouth and killed himself. As I grew up I figured he must have been chronically depressed, or worried about paying bills, or missed Italy and the family he left behind, or maybe, maybe—something I would never know. Oh, I prayed, don't let it be the Hershey bars I stole that did it!

In any case, I felt very bad for Mrs. Rizzo and I felt bad because they were Catholics and one of my Catholic schoolmates hissed into my ear that this was a Mortal Sin, meaning that Mr. Rizzo couldn't go to Heaven and I wondered what kind of God wouldn't let this very kind man into His Heaven. I didn't want Mr. Rizzo to have to carry the burden of sin into the next life.

Even if the Catholic Church, I figured, could not forgive a suicide, this Episcopalian would.

The Girl who Loved Box-ing

But before that, in more innocent times, when I was eleven years old, the Rizzo cellar held a treasure for me: cardboard boxes.

I wanted a dollhouse and there was a colorful metal two-story one in the window of the 5 & 10 Cent store. It had fake wallpapered walls and fake rugs on the metal floors. (When I recently saw one in an antique store my eyes started to tear up from the memory of the metal doll house I eventually received for Christmas—a most cherished possession)—but I had no idea my parents had heard my yearning for one; and I had to have one *now*.

So I found an empty cardboard box from somewhere and made a dollhouse from it. I borrowed (without asking my mother) a carving knife from the kitchen, and upstairs in the bedroom that Judy and I shared, first making sure I was alone, carefully sliced off the folding parts of the box.

Then I made slits in the center sides of the open box and slid the cut cardboard into the slits to make an upstairs and a downstairs, after I turned the box onto its side.

Invariably baby Johnny would find it, sit on it and crush it.

Then I found there were boxes in Rizzo's market! So I would hang around until either Mr. or Mrs. Rizzo emptied a box. Then I would ask if I could have it. They, figuring we were packing up quite a bit of something—("Are they moving without paying their bill, I hope not")—, started saving boxes for me. Sometimes Mr. Rizzo would even go down into the cellar and bring me up a box when he saw me coming.

This was the gold at the end of the rainbow! I became the cardboard dollhouse champ.

"Why are my carving knives so dull?" my mother wondered. I sat quietly with my book.

Then—*then*! One wonderful day Mr. Rizzo was too busy to go to the cellar to get me a box, so he told me I could go down there and get one myself. A little reluctantly I went down the stairs. But the cellar was clean and smelled like onions, not dirt, and I had my choice of an array of boxes—Boxes for three-story houses, for long houses, short houses—the sheer volume of boxes filled my soul. I started picking out my own boxes.

If the Rizzos wondered about me and my box fetish, they knew not to ask.

But this largesse had to cease. The Rizzos hired a high school kid to sweep out and do some general heavy lifting. I had a bad feeling about this the first time I asked him for a box and he went to the cellar and brought me up a box that didn't suit my needs. But I was too shy to ask for anything else. He was taller than me, pimply and his voice squeaked every now and then. He seemed to have no sense of humor.

I thought I was living my invisible life until one day I asked for a box and the high-schooler stopped sweeping, leaned on the broom, and looked me full in the face.

"What'd'ya do with them things—*eat* 'em?" he asked.

It was the end of my dollhouse-making career. That kid kept me from becoming a world-famous interior decorator.

✫ ✫ ✫

Me with old Friends. 1991.
Back: Mitch Kreher, Russ Vann, Jim VonBenken
Front: me, Charlotte Vann, Sally (Tolli) VonBenken

Their Dancing Daughters (and Sons)

Knowing how to play the piano brought me into worlds I hadn't known existed. This was in the days before television, so our view of the world was limited to the radio, newspapers, magazines and the movies.

None of these told me that there were little boys and girls (mostly girls—*very* reluctant boys) who put shoes on that had metal taps on the bottoms, and get out on a floor and tap.

I knew about dancing, of course. My mother played week ends with a dance band, and we went to enough Polish weddings to dance plenty of polkas.

But these were little (mostly, as I said) girls whose mothers sat in folding chairs around a big empty room with a wooden floor and huge mirrors and watched their children tap dance. I had the job of playing the piano and keeping up with the instructor's beat. Since I didn't need sheet music when I played, I could watch the kids' steps and the mothers' secondhand looks of yearning to dance, too.

Then in high school I got a job playing piano for some very rich and privileged children at a private school in New Britain. I hadn't known that such people or places existed outside of Hollywood and it was a jolt for me to realize that this was right here, right in the same town where I had been born. Well, actually, several miles and hundreds of thousands of dollars actually separated us.

The young junior-high school boys wore suits, shirts and ties and the young girls wore velvet, silk and satin. I"m sure I had my mouth open in awe much of the time. These were not people who were raised to loop springs! I was invisible to them in a way I was not used to. I saw that my I.Q. mattered not—just my connections. And I had none.

A matronly woman with eyes of steel ruled them and their dancing propriety. There was to be absolutely no fraternization and no boy was allowed to sit down while there was any girl who had not been chosen to be prodded around the dance floor. Money aside, plenty of junior high hormones were raging in those boys, evidenced by much jostling, and the matronly woman spent much of her time pulling them into line.

It's the first job I had where I was openly terrified of the boss.

To Work or Not to Work? That is the Question (for Women Back Then)

> "I miss the days when women were to be empty vessels for men's ambitions"—
> Mark's dad, <u>Doonesbury</u>—Garry Trudeau

In the 50s and 60s we women were expected to stay at home and manage things. Husbands/fathers brought home the money. Wives/mothers spent it. Men got a lot of mileage out of railing at women about their spending habits. Women got the same mileage out of hiding the bills from the men.

But something was missing, and it was Equality. Women felt diminished asking for "an allowance" from their husbands, as though they had exchanged one father for another; and men felt powerful, but distanced from the intimacy they wanted from their spouses.

Equal Rights for Women (E.R.A.) had to happen.

More to the point, my husband went through a dry spell in his own business and I could see that something was going to have to be different. With lunch money for the five kids in mind, I went to work at Tony's Italian Restaurant as his lunchtime waitress.

As his *only* lunchtime waitress.

Daughters Liz and Caroline had somehow discovered Tony and his wife Sharon, who offered them jobs in the restaurant kitchen, at the end of our street and across from the beach. Our daughters were 14 years old at the time—they loved the job and they loved Tony and Sharon.

I was fearful that the girls wouldn't have anything to eat and so I would pack dinners for them, complete with napkins, and bring them dinner every time they worked. Sharon loved the turkey dinners I made and she'd take those, the girls told me years later. They were amused that I packed them food and a napkin—food and a napkin to a restaurant!—and they never told me to stop doing this. In reality Tony was keeping them well stocked in Italian dinners.

Tony and Sharon fought often and publicly and then Sharon would run crying from the restaurant and Tony would run after her, yelling back to Liz and Caroline, "Girls—take over the kitchen!"

And they did. Did the patrons have any idea that young teenagers were cooking and serving up their dinners? And doing it quite well? And that the whole thing was probably illegal?

Liz and Caroline were the ones who told me about the daytime waitressing job. We needed the money and all the kids were in school, so this was a perfect time and place to work. I would go to the restaurant in the morning and prepare the salads. Used to working in my own kitchen, I would walk around with a carving knife in my hand while Tony reminded me to put it down.

Tony's lunches were excellent and they were inexpensive. There would be a pasta dish, salad and garlic bread—all for $1.49 plus tax. Figure then that my tip might be a quarter, and I would come home daily with enough quarters to keep the kids in lunches at school.

There was enough room in Tony's Venezia de Notte for 80 diners, and at lunchtime every day that's how many showed up.

I want to remind you again that I was the *only* waitress. And all 80 people had to get back to work inside of an hour.

At 1:10 pm I would stare at an empty room of tables filled with dirty dishes. Somehow I had served everyone, but I couldn't remember how. Eighty people in one hour, with my shoving orders at Tony, grabbing plates when he yelled, "Pick up!" and making sure the diners had drinks and the correct checks, taking their money, making change—it seems like a world ago.

One fall Saturday afternoon I worked a shift. The entire football team from Hoover Junior High came piling in. I took down their orders. Liz and Caroline were working in the kitchen and they called me in.

"Mom, is this *79* orders of pepperoni pizza?" one asked.

"No," I said, "that's the football number on the jersey, to keep the orders straight."

Their laughter followed me out of the kitchen.

One evening I worked a shift and got to see Tony at his fiercest. A patron motioned me to his table.

"Look what I found in my salad," he said, and held out a shard of glass. "Is *this* how you operate? I'd like a free meal for this."

Stunned, I took the piece of glass carefully into the kitchen and informed Tony. I watched as his face turned purple and he picked up a meat cleaver. I cringed against the wall, stunned, and pointed to the correct table.

Tony, cleaver held high, burst into the dining room. "I NO GOT-A GLASS IN-A MY KITCHEN!" he boomed.

The man paid for the meal.

✡ ✡ ✡

74 | Your End of the Boat is Sinking

Me, fifth grade.

PROOF OF GOD AND HIS/HER SENSE OF HUMOR

Dad Comes To Dinner

After Dad retired from Fafnir Bearing Company in New Britain, he and Mom sold the house we had all grown up in, and moved into a small one-bedroom retirement apartment. They both still smoked and the white walls turned yellow in no time.

Then Mom's dementia became more pronounced—she was found outside in her nightgown one cold evening, looking for McDonald's so she could get a fish sandwich, her favorite—and she repeated herself over and over, preventing any conversations with Dad.

When the smoke damaged Dad's heart and he needed surgery, my brother John, who lived the closest, assigned himself to move Mom into a nursing home, where Dad would join her temporarily while he recovered.

"Hardest thing I ever did, Barb," John told me later. "When the men came to take her to the Home she fought them and screamed higher and louder than I'd ever heard—it was an animal in pain." She was beyond reasoning with at this point, and any time Dad was out of her sight she became terrified.

Dad joined her after his stay in the hospital. By then she had trouble remembering who he, or we, were. There was a piano in the home and she loved playing it.

She could have become a concert pianist, that's how good she was. Dad told me that her music teacher wanted her to go to music school and then to become a professional pianist. But Mom was scared to go too far from home, so when I was young she just played in a local dance band on week ends. I loved studying the music sheets she brought home, accordions of pages ready to fan out along the music rack. She showed me music she had learned while taking lessons as a girl—I still can't play the intricate pieces she played.

Whenever I visited her in Connecticut from my home in Florida, I would trace her mental regression by the increasing simplicity of the songs she played—from Rachmaninoff, her fingers flying along the keys, to her brain spinning down to "Mary had a little lamb".

I would play duets with her. She enjoyed those and always smiled at me when we ripped through a song, but I don't think she knew who I was.

But if I don't tell you about this most-talented woman who was so fearful of life, whose fearfulness vanished as she played classical music every evening after supper, then I have not done her justice. She passed on some of her pianistic gifts to me and I am grateful for that, remembering Ruth Josephine Carlson Rackliffe almost every time I sit down at the piano and play.

After his surgery Dad tried to walk the length of the corridor from their room to the dining hall, but he was exhausted halfway there and asked John bring him a wheelchair. As he settled into it he said to my brother, "This is the first time in my life I've felt old."

He died four days later.

We brought him to Bailey Funeral Home, where Mr. Bailey's son Jim now ran it. Jim let us have a private viewing before other people were allowed in. We brought Mom from the nursing home and she stared at Dad's face and body in the open casket. John and I held our breaths, uncertain of her reaction. She hadn't known that he had died, although people had tried to explain this to her.

She stared and then she looked up at us.

"Who the hell **is** that?" she demanded. John and I, exhausted from the tension of bringing her here, laughed, since we'd never heard her swear anything worse than "Shoot!". Then she went to the casket and put her arm under his shoulders and told him, "Come on, Les. Come on home now." We were touched. This was the man who had cared for her for well over 50 years and five children.

Then we took her back to the nursing home and we went out to dinner, my husband, my brother John, his wife Pat, my sister Judy and her husband Ericke, and several grown grandchildren. We went to Cooke's Tavern, a Colonial carriage stop from the 1700s turned into a restaurant (where I had worked one summer as a cashier in my teens—I forgot to mention that job), and we spent the evening reminiscing about Dad and talking about Mom's welfare, while eating excellent food.

"Did you know Mom won a race last week? She was the fastest on the track of all the older people out there from the nursing home. Her photo was in the paper."

"She always liked to run," someone else remembered.

"Dad would have liked this," we all said over and over again. The night was a special one—for the first time in many years we were able to have conversations and tears and laughter without being constantly interrupted by Mom's questions, or her wanderings. We hadn't realized how much constant care she had needed and how Dad's watching over her had prevented us from talking with him until she wasn't with us.

"Dad would have liked this," we said again. We toasted our brother Tom, who had died of brain cancer just into his 34th year.

The check came. "This is from Dad's insurance," said John. "It wasn't much and he wanted it divided among us." He turned to me, his older sister. "Barb, you're so smart"—his running joke to me—" how much did the bill come to?"

Now I hadn't watched what anyone ordered, so I just dashed a number off the top of my head. I've forgotten now what the number was, but I saw John's eyes get huge.

"Was I close?"

"*To the penny*," he said.

I gasped and then raised my glass. "Thanks, Dad, for being here with us tonight," I said. Nobody else could have whispered that number in my ear.

All Roads Meet in Ocala

Husband Mitch and I have gone to a dental seminar in Gainesville. He is out of sorts because he lost a tiny screw from his glasses and without it the lens won't stay in the frame, so he can't drive us home without it, and he has reluctantly let me drive.

Now I am a good driver. In fact (and my own children will bear me out on this one) I am a better driver than Mitch is. His children probably think he is the better driver, but I haven't asked them.

So I am driving us home and Mitch sits in the passenger seat, veering between dozing and trying to help me drive.

What we have not counted on is that there has been a huge homecoming game in Tallahassee, and now we are in the midst of the Miami fans who clog the highway, so we are down to moving 20 miles per hour.

I put up with this for an hour or so and then pull off the highway onto a road into Ocala. We'll go the back way home, I've decided.

"What are you doing?" says Mitch, roused into an upright position.

"I'm taking a back way to get home, out of this traffic."

"We'll be out of it in no time," Mitch argues. But I'm off the highway now and as we look back to the north there is nothing but a solid line of cars.

We have lunch at a diner. Mitch desperately wants to drive, even half-blind. I keep a tight hold on the car keys.

Back in the Avalon we head east, where we'll join the road that goes south. I look at the car in front of me, and to my delight see that it has a Connecticut license plate. One of my pastimes in Florida, even after all these years, is to spot Connecticut plates.

I move a little closer and can't believe it! The car is from *Plainville*, my home town! It's even from the car dealer's that sold all the second-hand Buicks over the years to my Dad. What a coincidence and here— in the middle of Florida!

I pull up at the traffic light where we are to turn left. I am excited to see the Plainville car pull up to my right, to go straight ahead. And the light is red!

"Open your window! Open your window!" I yell at Mitch. I lean across him as much as I can with my seatbelt on.

"I'm from *Plainville*!" I call across to an elderly couple. They have their window open already.

"That's nice," says the man, without getting excited himself.

"My maiden name was *Rackliffe*!" I am deafening Mitch with my shouting.

"That's nice," repeats the man. His wife smiles at us. "When I was young, a lady named Rackliffe used to babysit me," he continues. "Now— what was her name?"

The light is about to change

"Ruth," he says in a mild tone of voice. "Ruth Rackliffe."

"That was my *mother*!" I shout, and now my eyes are filling with tears. What are the odds of finding in Ocala the very man who used to be babysat by my mother? Surely tougher odds than winning the lottery—

The light changes and we are on our way, they straight ahead and Mitch and I to the left.

"Well—!" is all I can say, rubbing the tears from my eyes. Mitch says nothing. "If I hadn't gotten us off the highway we would never have *met*!" I ponder wonderingly.

"That's true," says Mitch. "How many things had to fall into place for this to have happened?"

"Starting with the screw out of your glasses," I say. I am also saying, "Thank you, Lord, thank you, Lord."

I have a photo of my mother, young, smiling, looking to me like a young Ingrid Bergman. The photo is untitled. She is holding on her lap a youngster that I have never been able to identify.

Now at last, maybe I have.

Titusville Dream

"—and Joseph, warned by an angel in a dream—"

There are many references to dreams in the Bible, as the above words from Matthew 2:13 tell us. And Matthew wastes no time—he writes about dreams *five* times in just the first two chapters of his narrative.

I have several dreams I want to share. I call them "signpost" dreams, because the message seems to be "You're on the right track and I'm here with you."

Years ago I suffered badly from agoraphobia—literally, a "fear of open spaces". I think now that I was living with an overactive thyroid (undiagnosed) that kept me from gaining any weight and left me feeling panicky and nervous and shaky much of the time.

Our Episcopal Church decided to be part of a movement called "Faith Alive", which became quite active in the 1970s. This consisted of teams from various churches getting together at a particular church for a week end. The individual team members who chose to would share stories of their faith and encounters with God.

My husband Ron wanted to go, so I joined him—but I was not prepared to drive all the way up to St. Gabriel's in Titusville—to me, the end of the world *one whole hour away!*

I obsessed over this, oscillating from trying to be strong about it and fearing I would absolutely die from a panic attack if I were that far from home. If you have never suffered from these attacks, you will think they are all in one's head. If you have suffered from them, you will be nodding in agreement at this point.

How could I possibly hide my condition for a week end with strangers while living in a stranger's home? These panic attacks could come on in an instant, causing my heart to pound and making me need to walk around and get my breathing back to normal—all the while being sure I was going to die.

The night before we left, I had a dream: I was in a room not my own. I was at a window and, looking down, saw that I was on the second floor. I looked around and there was something yellow on the bed. There was a piece of furniture with a secret compartment.

The dream was vivid. It is vivid to this day. And with it came a sense of peace, so that as I remembered it the next day as Ron drove us to Titusville, I was not clutching the door handle with a sweaty right hand as often as usual.

Did you know that Titusville has *hills*? I didn't know that until we reached our hosts' house, which was a split-level. The welcoming couple took us to our room—on the second floor, and I went to the window and looked down, in awe because of the rarity of a split-level house in Florida at that time.

"Now how did *that* get here? I meant to have the room all ready for you," said our hostess, and she grabbed up a bright yellow bathrobe from the bed. I stared at the yellow fabric. Two out of three! Maybe the week end would be all right.

For some reason on Friday evening I was made the Music Leader of the Faith Alive team. I spent the week end teaching songs and doing gestures to "His banner over me is Love". I possibly had some panic attacks, but I don't remember them. And my fear was absent from Friday to Sunday.

On Sunday afternoon Ron and I were getting ready to leave. I found a letter in my purse. I forgotten to mail it. Ah— I had neglected to put a stamp on it.

I asked our host for a stamp. "I"ll pay you for it," I said, and he laughed me off by waving his hand at me. "In my desk, in a cubbyhole," he said.

I looked through his desk and couldn't find the cubbyhole. He was still smiling.

"It's a *secret* one," he said, winking at me. He pushed something on the desk lid and a little drawer jumped out at me.

And *that*'s a signpost dream.

Losing Chris

Christopher is the youngest of our five children. He was named for St. Christopher, "The Christ Bearer", a big sturdy man, and that is what I hoped for this son. I remember the pew I was sitting in when I opened the hymnal and there was the name "Christopher" and I knew it was the right name if this baby was a boy.

Chris was at home in the world. When he was not yet four years old, he wandered down the street on his tricycle. We mothers didn't worry about our children the way mothers have to nowadays. On our block we were all stay-at-home Moms and there was always someone out on our quiet street, where we counted 30 children total, to make sure the kids stayed in line.

He had already climbed a palm tree and walked around on our roof. He had learned to swim by watching a group of Girl Scouts learn to swim in our pool to earn their badges, and after they had gone home, had splashed into the pool to practice what he'd seen, so that he was swimming in the two weeks they were there.

He showed up now while I was hanging out clothes. "I went to school," he said. "I looked in the windows and saw the kids and I want to go to school." He described the school, which was down the block and around the corner another four blocks.

I phoned the school. "Was there a little boy on a tricycle at your school just now?"

I was told yes. "Do you have room for him?" Again, yes. So he started school. Every morning when the weather was good he mounted his tricycle and rode up the street. When he turned the corner and I couldn't see him any more, I phoned the school to watch for him. We repeated this routine at noon—the school phoned to say Chris was on his way. I put his lunch on the kitchen table and then went outside and stood in the street. At first I could hardly see him, and then he would come closer, pedaling furiously and singing the songs he'd learned.

Listen, I'm scaring myself as I write these words. Dr. Phil says the world has changed and is he *right*—I would never recommend today that my granddaughters send out their children like this.

He was about this age when I had a vivid dream that I lost him. I was searching frantically for him, when suddenly in my dream a very old man came to me and said, "He is safe."

The next day in reality I lost him. Only the dream I had had the night before kept me from total panic. The neighbors helped me look for him, and we found him across the near end of our street, across Riverside Drive, where traffic had been diverted because the road was being dug up for sewer lines. The road was now ten feet deep and full of sand that could cave in on a small boy. He had never gone this way before, and how he got across the road was a mystery. I didn't take his wanderings for granted after that, although he still rode his trike to school.

That old man must have guarded him. Angels come in many guises.

✲ ✲ ✲

The "Big Face" look. My children – Diana, Chris, Caroline, Jon, Liz.

The One-Armed Woman with the BB Ashtray

I took a morning class sponsored by Brevard Community College in the early '70s. It was for women, designed to help women with self-esteem and helping them to write resumes and practice taking interviews for jobs. It was called WENDI—"When Entering New DIrections".

But it was much more than that. It was a safe place where women could find their voices. It's hard now to realize that we didn't know who we were outside of our husbands and children. My name was Mrs. Ronald Willey. There was nothing of me, Barbara, in there, and I realized that if I died and Ron remarried, she would be Mrs. Ronald Willey, as though we had interchangeable parts. I was quite resentful in those days and I remember seeing a road sign: "Men At Work" and saying angrily out loud to myself, "*Women* work, too, you know!"

So the Women's program I was in was to help women get blue collar jobs, not just secretarial ones, jobs that would pay them more, jobs that would get them working side by side next to men. If this now sounds like ancient history, it wasn't that long ago.

I loved this class. We shared our lives! I'd never heard stories of women's struggles, of living with alcoholics, physically abusive husbands, runaway children—it would set me on the path to becoming a mental health counselor.

Apparently the woman who ran the class saw something in me, because after the class was ended, her boss came to me and asked if I would teach a class myself. A woman who was teaching had to have emergency surgery, the class had been scheduled, and would I take it over?

Uh-uh. No way, no how. I still had intense agoraphobia. The class that had just ended was only 10 minutes from home and I could handle that. But to be in charge of a class—to panic and not be able to leave the room? No. No. No.

My teenaged daughters were no help. "Sure, Mom, go ahead," they said, their eyes on a board game they were playing with their boyfriends—boyfriends who would be in the house Alone With My Daughters If I Took This Job. Uh uh. No. Nope. Never.

But something was compelling me to try it. So I drove to Cocoa for orientation, feeling panicky over being 25 minutes from home. Orientation consisted of heaping my arms full of books to help me get organized.

"Where will my classroom be?" I asked my preoccupied boss Lois. She waved me away. "Oh—someplace. There's no room on the Cocoa campus, so we've found you a classroom in a local church. You'll find it—don't worry."

Don't worry? At home I dumped the books on the bed and stared at them. What was I doing, thinking I could do something like this? This defied all rational thought! I needed to phone Lois, that's what I needed to do, and tell her No. No. Absolutely not.

But I didn't. And knowing I was going to work the next morning, I tried to sleep.

I finally fell asleep and this was my dream: I was at Sanibel, surely for me and my family the most relaxing place in our Florida world to be. But this time I was alone. At my feet I saw a bathroom scale and I stepped on it. It read "110".

I stepped off and there was a second scale. I stepped on it and it also read "110".

That was not my weight in real life. I was very skinny and probably tipped the scales at 105 pounds. But the dream was a calming one and I didn't have a panic attack until I was in the car the next morning, the passenger seat piled high with books, on my way to my first class. I had never taught before, except for piano students. This would be adults—my peers.

Somehow I found the church. There was already a ragtag group of women walking around, chatting, smoking. I got out of my car and a woman with only one arm came up to me. The other arm was gone below the elbow, and in the crook of that elbow she had wedged a BB-weighted fabric and metal ashtray. "You the Teach?" she asked breezily.

I nodded. "So where do we go?" she asked. The other women stared at me.

"I'll find out," I said and walked over to a little boy, whose father was mowing the church lawn. "I'll find out for you, lady," he said, and ran off to the church office.

He was back fast. "Ten!" he yelled over the mower sound.

Ten. That didn't sound bad. That was close to my dream of 110.

"Okay, thanks," I called back. "Ten."

"Not *ten*, lady," he yelled. "*One-ten*!"

One hundred ten. One hundred ten. I gathered my books and my women and we found classroom 110.

I taught women's courses for the college for the next 16 years. Long after that I would run into my "graduates". "You changed my life!" I would be told with a hug.

Fair swap. They changed mine.

✷ ✷ ✷

After a year or so I was given a class at the Melbourne campus, much closer to home. My friend Charlotte Vann and I took turns driving and talking. Since I am an extrovert and she an introvert, I got the better part of that deal. I would talk all the way to school and she would talk all the way (quieter and at a less machine-gun fire pace). I'm not sure if the teaching did me more good or if it was the friendship we developed from those drives. We were both getting our counseling degrees while we were teaching, so we had a lot in common.

One time I was teaching an Assertiveness class and a man and wife were among my students. The man was clearly defensive about being in this class and toward the middle of the first morning he challenged me: "Call yourself a teacher! Hah! Even that woman over there" (he pointed) "could teach better than you!"

I looked at the woman he had pointed out, and she was a student of a couple of my other classes. She was sharp and bright and people liked her.

"You know, you're right," I told him seriously, and to the woman I said, "How would you like to teach a class?"

The man jumped up and grabbed his grinning wife. They didn't come back.

✷ ✷ ✷

Another time we had a guest speaker. She was also my boss and I was wanting to make a good impression and show off my class of women.

Just before she arrived, one of my students, a huge muscle-y female, came in with an attitude. She had a large bandage around her forehead. We were all scared of her. "What happened to you?" one of the braver students asked.

"Don't wanna talk about it." We all wisely retreated from the subject.

My boss came in then and started to speak after I introduced her. At her first sentence, Muscle Lady stood up. "I wanna talk about it *now*," she boomed. My boss sat down.

"See, I was inna bar last night and this here woman showed up who wanted muh man. So I *shoved* her across the bar and muh man took a bar stool and hit me with it, to make me stop. So I goes home and comes back with muh gun and I fired a warnin' shot at him, which un-fortun-ately rick-shayed and hit him in thuh elbow."

She sat down. There was a heavy moment of silence.

"Who knew a bullet could rick-shay like that? " She paused. Then, triumphantly—"I got muh man back."

The Good Fairies of the Episcopal Church in Orlando

"Mom," eleven-year-old Liz shook me awake. "Mom!"

I turned to face my daughter. "It's Caroline. She's crying like she's been doing for the past three nights. She's hurting, Mom!"

"I haven't heard her crying," I said, as I put on a robe.

"She's been trying to be quiet about it and not bother anybody."

We went to Liz's twin sister Caroline's bedside, where Caroline admitted she'd been having very bad headaches. As soon as it was daylight I phoned the doctor and we hurried to his office.

He examined her and did some tests, finding a dark spot behind her eye. He took me aside.

"Barb, I've only seen this once in my life and it was cancer. You need to get her to the hospital in Orlando. I'll give you the name of the man to see. He'll want to do a spinal tap."

We made an appointment and my husband and I drove Caroline to Orlando. I was secretly terrified. I prayed on the way there, "Don't let anything happen to her—please, Lord."

Caroline was admitted and put to bed. Ron and I came into her room, prepared to stay with her, when suddenly a crowd of women looking very much to me like Disney's Good Fairies in "Sleeping Beauty" marched in and circled the bed.

"We're from the Episcopal Church in Orlando and we're here to pray for Caroline. You can go—we'll take good care of her." They shooed us out of the room.

The next day Caroline had tests, which showed that the darkness behind her eye was *gone*. I'd seen the original x-rays. There was to me only one way to explain it.

It's Very Quiet in the Sky When the Plane Runs Out of Gas

I've told this true story in my first book "I Could Always be a Waitress". Here it is in its entirety. I'd love to hear from you about any incidents you've had like mine:

By now my agoraphobia is not a secret. In a panic attack all the victim wants to do is get away and walk around fast to burn off crazy energy until his/heart comes back to normal. It is a most frightful feeling.

Husband Ron had a plane. Not a regular plane—this was a World War II Trainer plane, painted bright yellow. It had a single seat in front and a single seat in back. During WW II it was used to train rookie pilots.

It was extremely noisy and smelled of gas and oil. Ron had rigged up a speaker system so that when we wore ear phones, he could press a button and I would know he was going to talk to me. I could also press a button I had, to talk to him. Otherwise, even if we shouted, we could not be heard.

Ron loved to fly. He was licensed to fly with instruments alone.

I hated to fly. Picture having a panic attack at 6,000 feet and not being able to open the door and get out—that was me.

He traveled a lot and this particular trip was to Connecticut. Nothing else would have gotten me into the plane, but I did want to see my parents; so I arranged for a live-in babysitter for the five children and we headed out from Melbourne.

I had an Agatha Christie murder mystery, borrowed from the library, with me. I figured I could get deep into a book and somehow forget that I was flying.

We headed north, Ron in front, me in back with my book and my fears. Around South Carolina I saw a lever beside my left arm move. "What's that?" I called to him over the intercom.

"Auxiliary gas tank. I've decided not to set down at the next airport. I'm going on to the one after that."

"Okay," I said, and went back to my book.

At that moment there was what I can only describe as a "Voiceless Voice" in my right ear.

"You do not have enough gas," the "Voice" said. It was matter-of-fact and left no room for doubt. I sat up, alert.

Then I did the wifely thing and put what I had heard into a question: I signaled Ron and asked, "Do we have enough gas?"

"Of course," he said. "We're on final approach now."

A sudden stillness as the engine quit. A sudden heart-stopping realization that it is *very* quiet when an airplane is turned into a glider. I could see Ron's back and shoulders as he tried to milk a little more gas into the engine—we were going down!

Only the Voiceless Voice I had heard kept me from screaming. We hurtled down, thousands of pounds of now- useless airplane, at high noon onto U.S. Highway #301. Ron somehow maneuvered the plane onto the right side of the highway, going with the traffic. We bumped onto the road, bounced onto the median, mangled a tree into the propeller, crashed across the other side of the road with its traffic, which could see us, and landed in the woods.

We were uninjured. We climbed out of the plane. Ron tried to pick up papers which were blowing from his open briefcase. I clutched my shoulder purse and tried not to faint, although I wanted to. People came from all around.

"Are you okay?" they asked. "How did you avoid the high-power lines?"

I looked back to where someone was pointing—and gaped. Huge high-power lines stretched across the divided highway. There was no way we could have missed them. The road was full of cars. There was also no way we should have missed hitting a vehicle, and yet Ron had been able to stay steer us through all this.

A man from the airport we had been heading for drove us to the airport. I went into the ladies' room. "My God, what happened to you?" asked a woman. I looked in the mirror—my face was chalk-white.

"I got us on another plane," said Ron, waving tickets at me. Less than an hour later we were taking off in a commercial airplane. My teeth were chattering.

Ron looked at me. "Is anything wrong?" he said.

Four hours later I was sitting at my old family kitchen table across from my mother. She had left a stick of butter on the table and I couldn't keep my eyes off it, watching it grow soft on the plate. "I was in a plane crash today," I kept repeating. "Mom, I was in a plane crash." She didn't seem to understand. Ron had gone on to his business meeting.

The C.A.B. called it pilot error. Apparently the gas tank had not been topped off in Melbourne.

The airplane was considered a total loss. The man who had given us a ride to the airport was a mechanic and he bought it and repaired it so that it flew again.

At an airshow in New Jersey a year or so later five T-6's were going around a pylon and crashed into each other. The pilots all died. The yellow T-6 was one of the planes.

The Agatha Christie book was never recovered. I paid for the book at the library—the first time I'd ever had to do that.

Ron bought another plane like the yellow one—this time a blue-green Navy SNJ, also a trainer with a seat in front and a seat in back. It smelled like the first one.

✯ ✯ ✯

I have never heard the Voiceless Voice since then, although I have yearned to; and yet I *know* there is someone right at my ear at all times. I have asked myself why this Guardian Angel felt called upon to prepare me, and I feel certain I'll get my answer in the next life.

There's one other part to this: I don't know if there are out-of-body experiences, but I do know that I had a distinct impression of a hand underneath the plane, guiding it down. Was I out of the plane at that moment, watching? Or was it something I sensed?

Our children, hysterical, phoned us the next day. We were hoping to get back and explain to them before they found out, but they read about it in the newspaper. Apparently the national news wires had picked up the story.

We told about our accident to friends. Ron told it as a joke. I added that when the plane had come to a stop, his helmeted head had not moved and I feared he was dead. But then he turned toward me and said, "Well—get out of the plane, Stupid."

I got out of the plane. I figured he was calling himself stupid and I was just the one in the way. We both always laughed when I said the "stupid" part. So our audiences laughed, too.

I was careful about adding the Voiceless Voice part, out of concern that the story would not then be a light-hearted one. I should not have been so careful; I had been given a heavenly gift and I should have shared it with everyone.

Which is what I am doing now.

1966.
Our children: Jonathan, Diana, Christopher, Caroline, and Elizabeth.
Barbara and Ron Willey.
Indialantic, FL.

Jon and His Unworn Knees

Jonathan is our fourth child of five and first son. He had the Swedish towhead, Once someone asked his younger brother Chris if he was Jon. "No," Chris said, "he's the one with the white hair."

When Jon learned to crawl he did it with straight legs, never getting down onto his knees to move. He looked a little like a crab with his rear end up in the air, his hands and feet flat on the ground. He developed this gait so well that he was quite fast.

His three older sisters and I laughed to watch him race around this way. We'd even get down on the floor and try to do it ourselves.

We were next door visiting one day and I was chatting and counting heads at the same time. "One-two-three-four, one-two-three-four, one-two-three—". Where was Jon?

Jonathan was a little way from me on the grass. I headed after him to turn around, calling him at the same time. He looked over his shoulder and shouted a baby shout of joy, and began moving faster down the sloping knoll in front of the neighbor's house.

I started running after him and he was really moving now. Then to my horror I saw a truck coming up our quiet dead-end street. The driver had been distracted by something and was looking away from a frantic mother and baby, who was almost at the road now.

I saw that there was *no way for me to reach Jon in time!* My heart was pounding. This was all taking split seconds and yet I felt as though I was running forever. I yelled to the driver, who didn't seem to hear me. Jon, still laughing—what a game this is!—hurtled toward the truck.

All at once a car came the other way down the road. The driver saw what was happening and leaned hard on his horn. The truck driver looked up now and swerved into the lawn across the road just a few feet from where Jon was about to enter the asphalt.

I swooped Jon up and held him, waiting for my heart to calm down. My legs gave out and I sat down on the grass with the baby. The neighbor got out of his car, his face white. We were both shaking. I stood up and we hugged with the protesting baby between us.

"I *never* come home for lunch," he said, "I mean *never*! But something told me to come home today."

I didn't know this neighbor. In those days we knew children and mothers, not dads. I knew that he had four young daughters, that the family was Catholic, that he had a crucifix dangling from his car's rear-view mirror.

I thanked him over and over again. I'd like to know where he is today—I'd like to tell him how he'd be so proud of the boy he saved, who grew into a six-foot tall man who spent time in the military and Afghanistan and is a respected veterinarian married to a lovely woman named TraMi, whose parents saved *her*, escaping from Vietnam with her when she was two years old.

I'd like to tell him that he was our guardian angel that day.

✲ ✲ ✲

A few years ago I was walking on the Indialantic beach. The area, as usual, was deserted. I noticed two young women sitting on a blanket up near the dunes and busy talking; so busy that they didn't notice that the baby they had brought to the beach was crawling fast right into the ocean.

I ran the way I had toward Jonathan years before and grabbed up the baby inches before she could be dragged under by the waves. She was too surprised to cry. Hugging her, I brought her back to the two women. One of them took her from me rather roughly.

"Your little girl was about to go into the ocean," I said, panting.

The young woman actually scowled at me. "He's a *boy*," she said.

✫ ✫ ✫

Jon's paternal grandfather died of lung cancer at age 58. He had been a heavy smoker. Jon had never known him, but he heard all my warnings about the dangers of smoking.

I took three-year-old Jon to a store one day and outside sat an elderly man, smoking. Jon stared at him. "You're smoking a cigarette," he said.

The man smiled at the towheaded child. "That's right, sonny," he said.

"You're gonna die!" said Jon. I didn't apologize for him.

✫ ✫ ✫

When Jon was a young adult he rented a U-Haul and helped move his girlfriend into an apartment, which she was going to share with another woman who'd run away from an abusive man.

We all warned her to not let him know where she was going—but somehow she did, and the man showed up in the parking lot as we finished emptying the truck.

I was on the ground and Jon was in the driver's seat of the truck when this huge menacing man confronted us. "What the hell you think you're doin'?" he yelled.

There have been few times when I knew I was in mortal danger and this was one. I looked into his eyes and for the first time in my life I saw the look of evil. Not drugs, not alcohol—*evil*. It terrified me.

"Get out of here," I said, in the strongest voice I could use. "Get out before I call the police."

His attention turned from Jon to me, and he seemed baffled that a woman would talk to him. I saw the hesitation. "I told you to get out of here!" I said in a stronger voice.

I was praying inside, "Jon, don't get out of the truck. If you get out of the truck he will surely kill both of us. This is no time to defend me by being macho."

The aggressive man suddenly turned, snarling like a wild animal, and got into his car, shaking his fist at me. He drove away. I couldn't believe it. I grabbed onto the handle of the truck to keep from collapsing. My knees felt like jelly. This had only taken a few seconds, but time had seemed to stand still.

"Jon, thank heaven you stayed in the truck," I said.

"I thought you knew what you were doing as a therapist," he said.

A few months later Jon phoned to say, "Do you remember that crazy boyfriend? He killed himself. Drove 100 miles an hour up U.S. 1 and wrapped the car around a concrete pole. The police were chasing him."

I had only one question—"Was he alone?" Yes, was the answer.

Thank you, Lord. He had not taken anyone else with him.

Me with the kids at Cocoa Beach – Diana, Chris, Jon, Liz, Caroline.

How Did She Get Past Security With That?

(This was neighbor Dianne Boehler's question when I told her this story.)

My husband and I were on a plane headed for San Francisco, to visit his relatives. I tended still to be a white-knuckle flyer. We landed in Dallas, and then boarded another plane to complete the trip.

About halfway there I noticed a drip-drip-drip coming from a compartment two rows ahead of us. Alarmed, I watched it for a while and when it didn't stop, called a stewardess.

"Might there be a problem with the air conditioning?" I asked her, pointing to the drips.

Or the engines or something else and are we about to crash at any moment? I wanted to say.

The stewardess opened the overhead compartment, but found nothing amiss. "Does anyone have anything leaking in here?" she asked the passengers. They all shook their heads. "It's all right," she soothed, patting my hand.

Lady, I wanted to say, *I was in a plane crash once, so I <u>never</u> think everything's all right!*

But my husband was dozing beside me, so I sat back, not wanting to look like the only fearful one on this plane.

Until the smell. *Now* there was a kind of an acidic odor coming to me. I sniffed the air. Couldn't anyone smell that besides me? Nobody else seemed alarmed.

I told my husband. "Barb, the stewardess said everything's all right. So it is." I didn't protest but I decided to keep a watchful eye on the drips. I memorized where the escape routes were. Nobody would be prepared except me, and I would probably need to help others—those ninnies with bad eyesight and worse senses of smell. Hah! Once they were safely on the ground and I was surrounded by reporters and people shaking my hand— *then* they'd believe me

Do *bombs* smell like acid? I guess they could. *Oh, they'll all be glad I was on this flight with them, when they're all rescued from certain death!*

So I talked to myself, on ready alert now, into San Francisco.

When we came to a stop and stood up to get our suitcases, a little old woman in a black shawl asked someone for help getting her parcels from the overhead bin two seats ahead of ours. One of the bags was wrapped in aluminum foil and now the acidic smell was overwhelming. "What **is** that?" I asked.

She turned to me, "Pot roast."

"*Pot roast?*" I repeated, stunned

"Pot roast. I bring to my daughter. I marinate, so it's ready to cook when I get to her house." The old woman now smiled at me, showing an absence of a few teeth. "She *love* my pot roast."

✲ ✲ ✲

Racing with the Moon

This is, thankfully, a funnier plane story than the T-6 one. Liz is old enough that she thinks it's funny, too:

An eclipse was going to take place in the north part of Florida and into Georgia and South Carolina. Ron, being the telescope expert that he was, wanted to see it. So he rented a seven-seat Cessna airplane for our family. We headed up to Tallahassee.

Tallahassee is a pretty long hop in a small airplane for seven people, especially when one decides to have a sulking fit. I use those two words "sulking fit" deliberately. The ""sulking" part is attitude—"I'm not going to tell you what's bugging me" and the "fit" part includes a lot of physical body language that gets into everyone else's space. And since we had three teenaged daughters and two younger sons, we could count on the strong possibility of someone's taking something personally and behaving irrationally.

In a small plane there's just not enough room for teenage behavior.

It was Liz's turn for sulking. Ron announced, "They're socked in, in Tallahassee. We won't be able to see anything. So we'll go on to Georgia."

If he had announced that he was going to throw us all out of the plane, Liz could not have reacted with more elbows and knees. "Ow!" the siblings on either side of her protested. At least in a car you can pull over to the side of the road and everyone can get out and separate for a bit. Not when you're at 6500 feet.

"You *promised*, Dad! You *promised* we were going to Tallahassee!"

"Liz—we can't see anything from there. Be reasonable. And quit kicking the back of my seat!"

But you can't get a teenager to turn reasonable just because you've asked. So we endured an angst-filled airplane ride to a small airport in Georgia, where we all thankfully got out of the plane and stretched.

Not Liz. She refused to leave the plane. She didn't know how to fly a plane, but Ron took the keys with him anyway.

And *there* was the eclipse! The sky became an eerie yellowish-gray color. It was a unique experience. We all would have been excited, except that we all knew the same thing: we had to get back into the plane and somehow make it through a trip home.

When we got back to our home airport Ron and I cleaned out the plane. That's when I found a crumpled-up piece of paper. It was in Liz's handwriting and it read, "HI, BEA, LOOK UP!!! WE'RE IN THE PLANE OVER YOUR HEAD!!!"

It was then that I realized that Liz's friend Bea was in Tallahassee and Liz had decided what a cool joke it would be to drop this piece of paper on Bea's head from 4000 feet—what a surprise!

You sure you know what your teenagers are thinking?

You have no idea.

✭ ✭ ✭

Animal Quackers

This is all I knew about farming—when I was young Dad had a Victory garden in our back yard and he helped me plant carrots. I kept pulling them up to see if they were big enough yet. He grew delicious tomatoes without needing to spray for bugs and I discovered that the finest taste in the world was in picking a tomato off the vine and biting into it, still warm from the sun. People who have done that will know what I mean. People who think tomatoes come from Publix will not.

I was married for just eight years to Glen, who was a family doctor 13 years older than me. We divorced amicably and he even stayed my grown children's doctor.

(For those of you counting, I was married to Ron for 23 years, Glen eight, and Mitch 20. That adds up to over 50 years, just not consecutively.)

Anyway, when Glen and I were first married he brought me one day to what looked like an abandoned house far south of Melbourne. He stopped the car in front of a tall chain link fence. It had a gate with a rusting lock on it. There was no driveway—you drove through grass to get to the garage and the front porch. There was a pond in front. The house looked as though it had been built by an amateur builder, more for function than style.

I hated it.

Excited, he said, "I've dreamed of owning this place for years. When I had the money the house wasn't for sale. When it was for sale I didn't have the money. Now finally I can buy it."

The property consisted of five acres. There were no other houses in sight. We got out of the car and walked around without a problem, since the metal fence only edged the road in front. We peered in through the windows. I got a glimpse of some dreadful swirly greenish-yellow wallpaper in the living room.

I removed those swirls as soon as we moved in. It turned out to be wallboard, the kind you would find in a mobile home, and was glued on with such a tough cement that it ripped the sheathing underneath. I saved a piece of the green swirl as a reminder of how nauseating the walls had been.

The saving grace was that the kitchen was up to date and there was a 30 foot by 30 foot screened porch with a roof off the kitchen.

My car was a truck and the first day I came by myself with a load of boxes to the deserted place, a couple of wild boars wandered into the yard. I jumped onto the bed of the truck. I didn't know how high a mean wild boar could climb, but I guessed not as high as the roof of the cab, if I needed to get up there. The boars paid no attention to me as they rooted their way onto the rear of the property

Glen bought a bright red riding mower. This was something I could do: cut all the grass while sitting. The first time I tried it, while Glen was at work, I found it rather relaxing. All I had to concentrate on was the path I was making. I had made a few rounds when out of the corner of my eye I spotted a cow grazing on the newly-cut grass. Now what was a cow doing in our yard and where had she come from? I kept mowing, watching the animal and suddenly realized this was no cow—it was a *bull* and it was coming at me and the red mower!

I shoved the gear into "high", a little faster than I could run, and I made it into the garage and got the door shut before the bull caught up with me. I sat back down on the mower and shook.

This became a family joke, Barb mistaking a bull for a cow! Everyone hearing the story discounted my terror. But I knew that if anything had happened to me, nobody would have known—nobody was around. And nobody wore cell phones back then.

After the mower the first thing Glen did was to buy six Mallard ducks, sex unknown. They were a day old, tiny yellowish-brown handfuls of fuzz.

I had decided to make the best of things, and I had read that you can imprint ducks to believe that you are their mother if you do it within 72 hours—so I took care of their feeding and indeed, they started following me around.

There's a photo of me standing at the stove. You can't see my slippers because they are covered in baby ducks, all peeping at me. In one of those ironies of life, I am scrambling eggs like a Florida cannibal.

As the six ducks got a little older, my routine would be to get up in the morning and go to the screened porch where they slept. "Duckies," I would say, and they would peep at me, their necks bobbing with (what I guessed) was joy, " Duckies! Want to go to the pond?"

They would then line up like those catered-to ducks in the high-priced hotel in Orlando, and walk through the house and out the front door that I held open for them, to spend the day in the pond and the front yard. As they got older and developed colored feathers so that we could tell the males from the females, they would swim in the pond with a bead of water caught in their backs at the neck, the water shining like a jewel.

The first time I saw them mating I was appalled: the male grabbed the female by her neck with his bill, held her head *under water* until her rear end bobbed up, had his way with her, then released her. She would come up protesting and shaking her head. I figured she was angry, because who wouldn't be?

I brought them out through a side door one day and that was a costly mistake, because the door slammed shut in the wind and caught one of the ducks in the neck. I picked it up and held it, crying and apologizing, until it died.

Okay, I know it was just a *duck*—but I was a very responsible mother. There is no way I would have made a good farmer's wife.

That evening after Glen came home and we buried the duck, we sat in the living room watching television. It was a pleasant evening and we had the doors and windows open. Suddenly the five remaining ducks waddled in and sat heavily at my feet. All I could figure out was that they too were mourning and needed their mother.

The first time they flew was comical. They walked around flapping their wings and at some secret signal from their brains and bodies took off one at a time, circling the roof of the house and the pond while looking down with what I thought were bewildered looks—"what the heck am I doing up here?"— at me, their mother, who was cheering them on.

They disappeared one by one over a period of the next weeks. I hope they migrated, but my fear was that the foxes that came through our property took them. I never wanted to know.

✣ ✣ ✣

Glen went to the feed store and bought a new batch of ducks, but these were older than 72 hours and acted like a gang of rebellious teenagers, although still small and downy.

One of them caught a cold and I got medication (for a duck!) to make it better. I wrapped it in a hand towel and brought it to my office with me.

That day as I saw clients in my mental health practice, I explained to them that I had a baby duck by my side, keeping it warm with my body while I worked with my clients. The duck would "peep-peep" every few minutes and I would say, "It's ok," and the duck would settle down until the next "peep-peep".

I didn't ask my clients what they thought. They seemed interested, but I could picture them going to a bar afterward and saying, "You know what kind of crazy therapist I have—?"

I killed two water moccasins on that property that were threatening my grandchildren, who had come for lunch. "Grandma, Grandma!" they yelled , "there's a gigantic snake out here!"

I grabbed the oversized ax I kept in the garage and ran outside to see the largest, nastiest water moccasin I had ever seen. These snakes are known for their bad tempers and aggressive behaviors. "Stay back!" I ordered the kids, and took a swing, killing the snake. I was shaking.

I went into the house, warning the kids to stay away from it, and as soon as I was in the house they were screaming again: "Grandma! There's another one!"

I killed that one, too. By then my adrenaline was pumping so furiously that I would have killed any other beast that I came upon, to protect my family.

✭ ✭ ✭

This second set of ducks refused to come in at night. They were certainly less tame than the first flock and they ignored my "Come on, duckies" call. They disappeared, too. I hope they all flew away.

Glen was working in town full-time. My practice was a part-time one and I kept making excuses to get away from that creepy house and land. I was invited to a brunch one day by a friend and I willingly went, meeting some new women in the process. Halfway through the morning to my surprise I started to cry.

"I don't know what the matter with me is," I sobbed, embarrassed in front of these strangers. This was so *not* like me!

"I do," said one. "You're living in a house that has bad spirits in it."

How did she know? I hadn't said anything about my house.

"Here's what you do," she said sympathetically. "My friends and I are psychics—" here several women nodded their heads—"and you are being worn down and you need them to leave. So you get garlic cloves and salt, and place a garlic bud in each corner of each room in the house. Then take the salt and make a ring of salt around the outside of the house. But leave the ends open so the spirits can get out! And I'll give you some prayers to say to get them to leave."

I felt better that I was being validated, even though I didn't do any of what I had been advised to do. Instead, I went home and started writing a book about the house. I never finished the book, but I felt a lot better. I bought my first gold cross on a gold chain, and wore it around my Episcopalian neck constantly. My husband, who was an atheist, frowned, but I didn't care.

For his part, he bought a little old used trailer and set it up toward the back of the property. He promptly filled it with chickens. Then our lives revolved around his chickens: we couldn't go to a movie in town because it would get dark and the chickens would be outside and vulnerable. In the daytime they scattered and we couldn't herd them inside the trailer.

Our sex life devolved to Fridays from 9 to 9:15 am, because he had to take care of the chickens. You probably don't know how hard it is to keep a man's attention when he's thinking about chickens. Protesting did no good: people could wait; chickens could not.

Chickens were, I decided, common. Mallards were more intelligent and regal.

We divorced a year after this, and I think in large part it was because of that isolated place where we lived. I drove past it a few months ago and it looked as God-forsaken as it ever had been. Glen lived in it for years after we divorced, with a new wife who gave the guest room, which I had restored meticulously, to her cat.

Last month, to get it finally out of my system, I wrote a one-woman one act play about the house—my last-ditch writing to get it out of my system. I sent it to a few friends for their criticism.

"Creepy", "scary", "weird" were a few of their comments. I know. I was writing from first-hand experience.

Monkey Business

I said that I would say more about the next-door Bailey monkeys, so I will: the first monkey that appeared was Buster. He was a Capuchin and he knew how to bite! He was a brownish color with a crew-cut look to the top of his head. Mr. Bailey had a special room rebuilt at the entrance to the kitchen, with bars on the windows and a barred door (I think. This may not be accurate. But at least there was a window in the door and it was barred.)

Buster was fast as a cat. Put your fingers too close to the cage and he'd grab them before you could say, "Think fast!"

We kids probably all had a turn getting bitten. We didn't worry about infection in those days, although we probably should have. A bite was a bite and a lesson to keep our distance.

(To people who have romantic ideas about taking care of a wild animal, I would just say: "GET REAL!" Taming King Kong only happens in movies.)

Mr. Bailey went to New York City and returned with an old-fashioned crank organ on a stick. It looked like a collector's item.

Then Mrs. Bailey made Buster a little vest and cap and a matching outfit for her husband. Buster, on a chain, would be quite an attraction as Mr. Bailey turned a handle and tinkly music came from the organ box-on-a-stick.

We kids were playing in the yard one day when the fire whistle blew. Now Mr. Bailey *loved* to go to fires. He was one of the town's volunteer firemen, and when we saw him head for the station wagon, somebody yelled, "Can we go, too? We wanna go!"

"Hurry up, then!" he called back and a half-dozen of us kids piled into the back of the station wagon. There were no seats there and we clung to the open window frames. I noticed that the organ was in the back with us.

Mr. Bailey hadn't put the tailgate up, and as he rounded the first corner on two wheels, we held on the best way we could, and saw to our horror that the organ was sliding on the slick wood floor of the beach wagon right out the back!

We yelled, but he thought we were just making noise until he heard us screaming, "The organ! The organ!" Then he stopped. The organ was sitting in the street, somewhat banged up. Fortunately no cars had hit it.

"Why the *@%& didn't you kids hang onto it?" he roared. We all shrank back, all of us knowing it was his responsibility and yet not daring to tell this to a furious adult. Fortunately, the sight of the fire engines pulling out from the station diverted his attention.

Buster was not the Baileys' only monkey. After a while they acquired a couple of gray spider-type monkeys, a female and a male. These monkeys had the run of the house and the male liked to sit with his back to the floorboard in the living room and show off his male appendage, which was usually at full-mast.

I applaud Mr. Bailey for not trying to apologize for his monkey, so we kids just looked at it as a natural occurrence. I think, however, at one point, Mrs. Bailey was able to get diapers on the little gray animals.

We didn't even have a cat or a dog! And they had *monkeys*! We didn't know whether to be envious or relieved.

My mother was soft hearted about stray cats. We'd find one licking the cream that had risen on cold mornings, from the bottles the milkman had left for our house. The cream would pop up with the cap from the bottle stuck to its top and this would attract cats.

She would eventually let them into the house out of the cold and then she'd get down on all fours, sniffing the baseboards and saying, "I just know a cat's been in here!" That's how I learned that male cats, especially non-neutered ones, smell differently from other forms of cats when they relieve themselves.

I had several canaries. They sat in a cage on a metal stand and it was my job to keep the floor of the cage clean with fresh newspaper, cut with scissors into a circle that would fit. I wasn't close to them—they were, after all, birds—but I enjoyed listening to them sing. And they were mine, bought with my birthday money.

Invariably I would come home from school and find that a cat had knocked over the birdcage and the birds would be gone—killed or escaped. This was very hard on me and I didn't want to go to school and leave my unwary birds behind.

It took me a long time to get over my animosity about cats and their predatory natures.

Judy, however, did not share these feelings. "I found a cat!" she called us one day from the back yard. "It's black and white and it's so beautiful!"

We looked outside. She was following a skunk across the back yard lawn.

My best buddy now is my cat. She's independent, as I am, and does not cuddle easily. I can pick her up for a few minutes before she struggles to get down. She purrs loudly when I scratch her. When we lived in Palm Bay she was very good at bringing snakes and lizards into the house through her cat door. I tried to appreciate these gifts and give her plenty of attention for it before dumping the creatures back outside.

She helped me discover the Joy of Cats. Thanks, Kitty.

I Run Away to Join the Circus

On July 6, 1944 a carelessly thrown cigarette caused the great Ringling Brothers Barnum and Bailey Circus fire in Hartford. One hundred sixty-eight people lost their lives and many more were injured. I knew of one girl in my school who died. I knew a kid with the scars of the fire on his body. Nobody teased him about it.

Circus people have huge superstitions and one of them is to *never again* play in a place where a tragedy has occurred; and that is how the circus ended up in a large field on the outskirts of my hometown Plainville.

I was probably eleven or twelve, still in elementary school. I determined to see the circus train come into town, and as was my usual way of operating, did not ask permission to get up at 4:00 am and leave the house unnoticed in the dark to go with a swarm of people to the center of town, to the railroad station close to the Strand Theater.

There was an excited hush to the crowd, except for the boys who rode their bikes in and out of the lines of people in the street. We were so thrilled to see what was about to happen that we didn't use the sidewalks! There were no cars in the road, just people, and mostly boys and men.

I wasn't afraid. This was my town and I was going to see the circus!

Some people had flashlights and when the train pulled in, shone them on the giraffes and the elephants. The elephants were the workers and lumbered down the train ramps. The smells were foreign and acrid, intoxicating and full of a hay and excrement aroma.

On foot as the sun rose we followed the elephants and the circus vehicles up the road, past the library and out of town a couple of miles to Tinty's Field, where the circus would be held (years later there would be a racetrack and a drive-in movie there also). I wouldn't have enough money for a ticket, so I was determined to see as much as I could for free. The boys on bikes rode fearlessly through the elephant poop in the road, daring each other to follow.

I wandered around, full of the wonder of it all. As the tents were being hoisted, the biggest boys on bikes were enlisted to carry water for the animals. Sawdust was everywhere. I was at the edge of the main tent when the poles were hoisted and the Big Top rose into the air, which was intoxicating with its shouts and smells and sounds.

I had not thought to pack any water, and as the morning grew hotter and I watched, avid to take it all in, trying not to even blink and maybe miss something, I blacked out in a faint and found myself on the ground with sawdust on my back.

Some people helped me up and got me a drink of water. A kind man with a truck drove me home. I'd never fainted before and I was embarrassed about this, since my life pattern was not to draw attention to myself.

Nobody in the family had yet missed me and I was able to get into the house unnoticed, except for my younger brother blabbermouth Tommy, who wrinkled his nose and said, "Pee-yew! What happened to *you*?"

The Circus. The Circus. I visited the Circus Museum in Sarasota as an adult and it brought back all my childhood visions again. I did get to go to the circus a few years later with a date, but it was not as good as my first memories, which were all tied up with being on my own and adventurous.

I need to remember that I once did this, as I grow older.

Organ Notes

A date took me rollerskating once when I was a teenager. I'd never gone to a rink, and what grabbed my attention was the *organist*, her fingers flying across the keys while she smiled at the skaters. I was hooked. I wanted that job more than I'd wanted anything much in my life.

Less than a decade later I was mostly through my junior year at Boston University when our twin daughters were born. Maybe I could have gone back to school with a single baby, but two took me out of the running completely.

I wouldn't have thought to complete my education years later had not General George Schlatter in our choir nagged at me to do so. I had five children and was playing the organ on Sundays, so I used that paycheck and the money I earned by giving piano lessons to go back to school.

I earned a Master's Degree this way, credit by credit, pupil by pupil, anthem by anthem.

Ten years before this I had seen an ad in the Diapason Magazine about a church in Winter Park, just outside Orlando, selling their pipe organ. I was curious and so husband Ron and I drove to the church to see what this was all about.

The church was selling a three-manual Austin organ (built originally in Hartford, Connecticut) so that they could replace it with a newer model. It had over 1500 pipes, from teeny to sixteen feet tall. We would have to remove it ourselves.

I didn't give the pipes any thought when I sat down at the console and played it. This was fun!

"Ron," I called, "we need to get this."

He answered me from twenty feet up in one of the two organ chambers, "Barb, there's a little more to it than you would think...."

It was daunting. *I* would have said no, but Ron loved a challenge.

First we had to take all the pipes apart. This took many trips to Winter Park over the week ends, with amused friends taking the children for us. We also had to have a room built onto the house that would fit the two organ chambers (airtight rooms big enough to stand up in) and then we would need three-phase electric power to get the thing going. Our home did not have three-phase power, so the power company was called in and Ron installed a huge generator-converter.

There was a pipe running under the new concrete floor in the new organ room, between the two chambers, and Caroline confessed to me years later that her Dad had persuaded her to crawl through the pipe to make sure it was unobstructed!

Then the pipes had to be fitted individually onto the top of the chambers, in specific order. We weren't done yet—we took apart the console and sent the pieces of chestnut to Mr. Farmer, the furniture finisher in town, who scratched his head at this puzzle he was being given.

When the console was completed and the pipes were standing up correctly and the power was on and the carpet had been cleaned because a sudden rainstorm had drenched the living room, since the roof had not yet been completed over the new organ room—then came The Tuning.

This consisted of my sitting at the console and playing two notes an octave apart, at a time. Ron was up in one of the chambers, moving cuffs up and down on the metal pipes to change the pitch, or opening and shutting metal pieces that looked like rolled-up open can lids on some of the wooden pipes for the same result.

We decided by the air currents if a pipe was tuned or not. The sound wanted was not "waaaaaw-waaaaaw-waaaaaw", but "waw-waw-waw" and most of our week end consisted of our disagreeing about when a pipe was or was not in tune. Nowadays there's no problem tuning a pipe organ—it's done with electronics—but back then we relied on our ears.

We had a stream of curious neighbors dropping by, grownups and children alike. When the work was all done, we held a carnival for a local cause and people took turns "playing" the organ for a nickel a turn.

We weren't through: I found another ad in the organ magazine— "Ron, here's another Austin pipe organ— in Winter Garden. 'Free—remove it yourself' !"

This time Ron and a group of men from St. John's Episcopal Church did just that, installing it in a new room built just for the pipes. It's still there and playable, almost 50 years later.

Go see it. It's in Eau Gallie. Check out the pipes. Tell them Barb sent you.

I actually did play in a dance band called "The Has-Beens". I played keyboard and Ed was on drums. There were two electric guitar players and we could really go to town with "Sittin' on the dock of the bay" and "Bad bad Leroy Brown".

We played at Moose halls and VFWs in the area. I think we were quite good. I wish we'd recorded us for posterity.

In those days smoking was all the rage—indoors and out— and although I was a sermonizing non-smoker, I would come home with my lungs and clothing saturated with the odor of Chesterfields. Even the next morning when I played the organ for the church service, I would still be exhaling cigarette smoke.

We played one New Year's Eve at a Moose lodge out of town. Boy, I looked good! I was at my fighting weight and my hair hadn't even thought of going gray. I didn't really need my glasses. In my long black sparkly gown I was the sexy member of the band—although one of the two male guitar players was really good-looking.

"Remember—don't go up those stairs," one of the band members told me at break.

"Why? What's up there?" I asked, curious now.

"Up there is where they have their secret meetings. No women are ever allowed. *Ever.*"

So of course I waited until nobody was looking and I sneaked up the stairs to the most secret domain of men only, no women allowed.

It was a room. Just a room. No windows. Just chairs around the perimeter and plenty of sad-looking stuffed moose heads on the walls.

I had stormed the boys' clubhouse and I was rather sorry I had.

And I wondered who cleaned the room. Did a cleaning lady come and have to wear a bandanna over her eyes, so she wouldn't see what was in there? Or did the men themselves clean the room?

I left that question to my fantasies, unanswered.

✧ ✧ ✧

Two other jobs I had: when women were allowed to be elected to the vestry of the Episcopal Church, I was the first one elected at St. John's in Eau Gallie, where I was playing organ.

I went to the first meeting determined *not* to make coffee for all the men, since this was an Equal Rights era and I was representing all forward-thinking women!

And then I was quietly taken aback when I found out that they already knew how to make their own coffee.

The other was when I was asked to run for the Indialantic Town Council. I had no idea how local politics worked, and not a lot of interest, either—but I was persuaded that the town needed me. And so I was elected—for a dollar a year. (A silver dollar—I still have it. It's glued to a plaque.) I filled out someone else's term. Now, I have voted in every election since I was of legal age, but as for making laws, I had no interest. I was relieved when the year was up. Possibly the town was, too.

The Austin pipe organ that we reassembled in our home.

Miscellaneous Musings

Daughter Diana and I travel well together, when it's just the two of us. As a youngster who was always in her older twin sisters' quite- extroverted shadows, I got to know her better as an adult. By this time she was a computer expert and had become a Labrador Retriever "Mom" for a series of those dogs. We have opposite personality types (I know about this—I was a mental health counselor), so what I am strong in, she is not, and vice versa.

Husband Mitch flew to Hawaii with his son to visit his daughter, who was stationed there with her husband and family. I didn't want to fly all that way, but after Mitch made his arrangements I didn't want to stay home, either.

So Diana and I decided to go up to New England, rent a car, and travel around to places I had spent time in as a child, like Connecticut, Boston and Cape Cod. I drove. She sat in the passenger seat with the road maps and our cell phones.

We approached Providence, Rhode Island at rush hour in the afternoon. The roads had somehow changed since I'd been there over 30 years ago, and we were both concentrating hard on staying alive— when my cell phone rang.

It was Mitch. He wanted to let us know, in long, drawn-out sentences, about what he was doing in Hawaii.

I was sweating. "Diana, just throw the cell phone out the window," I swore. Traffic kept closing us in. Mitch kept talking—I could hear his voice, all the way from Honolulu.

I told you Diana and I are different personalities. I would have been kind. Not Diana.

"Gotta go, Mitch," she said and hung up. She didn't answer when he called right back.

We both concentrated on not dying in Providence.

We parked atop one of the hills and walked around. Walking back and forth was fine and even going downhill was not a problem, but when we started *up* again toward the car, we were both winded in no time.

"We're—puff puff— used to flat ground in Florida," I reminded Diana. She nodded, too out of breath to reply.

An old man moved briskly past us, also going uphill. He wasn't sweating or panting.

"Maybe we're doing it wrong," I suggested. Of course! There had to be a *correct* way to walk these 45 degree slopes.

We found that the best correct way to do it for us Floridians was to drive.

✣ ✣ ✣

Once I won $300. I consider this about the most money I ever made for having something of mine published. <u>Reader's Digest</u> paid me for an anecdote, printed it, and here it is:

My daughter Caroline, an identical twin, had identical twin daughters, April and Stacey. One day when they were toddlers I babysat them.

"You can give them a bath, Mom," said Caroline as she left. "They like that."

"But once I get their clothes off, I can't tell them apart." This was true.

"Ask Rick—he knows how to tell them apart." Rick, the six-year-old. Okay—kids knew things like that, I was sure.

So I undressed the toddlers and gave them a bath, then wrapped them in towels.

"Okay, Rick," I called him. "Which one is which?"

He didn't lift his eyes from the TV set. "It's easy, Grandma,." he answered. "April always wears blue."

Mitch, a Prosthodontist (that's a specialist in restoring teeth), needed a front desk person. I had burned out from taking care of borderline clients ("*I love you, Barb! No I don't, I hate you, Barb!*"—*they really feel that way*) in my practice and was ready for a sabbatical.

"Just come in for a few hours a week and answer the phone," he urged.

So I did. And spent the next ten years there. I dwindled my practice down, referred the rest of my clients out, and settled in to be The Woman Behind The Man. I learned a lot about dentistry and the numbering of teeth and how to run x-rays through the processor. I told Mitch, "I will never argue with you in front of the patients," and I never did. When I had to assist him chairside and things got tense, I would whistle softly into my mask.

My mental health skills came in handy. When we talked with a new patient I would see things from that person's point of view and start asking the doctor questions that I thought needed to be answered. This drove Mitch crazy for about a year until he got used to it.

I hired daughter Liz to do the computer work and the billing and we made a powerful team at the front desk. We were both new to dentistry, so no question posed by a patient was too trivial for us to want an answer, too.

Our hairdresser's studio was just across the street. This made things handy for Liz and me to take turns getting haircuts, and one day when an older woman with a bouffant hairdo was in the chair, being fitted for a crown, I called my hairdresser to see if she could see me. She could.

"Hold down the place, Liz," I said. "If Mitch wants to know where I am, tell him I'm in the bathroom. I'll be right back."

I was back in 20 minutes. There was no Mitch, no patient. Liz was laughing in an odd way and frantic at the same time.

"The patient moved and knocked the crown out of Mitch's hand. We searched the place on our hands and knees, but couldn't find it. The patient says she didn't swallow it, but she's getting senile and we couldn't take any chances, so Mitch has driven her to the hospital for an x-ray. Oh—and he wants to know why you were in the bathroom all this time."

Chastened, I told her I would let the patient's sister know when she came to drive the patient home.

"How will you break it to her?" Liz asked.

"I'm a mental health counselor. I can do this carefully."

The sister returned a few minutes later and I said fast, " Here's what's happened: your sister's not here. Dr. Kreher lost the crown and thinks she may have swallowed it, so he's taken her to the hospital for an x-ray."

Liz stared at me: *this is how you break it to someone carefully*?

The patient's sister burst out laughing, surprising both of us. "Things sure do happen to her," she said, wiping her eyes.

No crown was found in the patient's windpipe or lungs. The crown was never found and a new one was made. Mitch very cautiously fitted it in place.

We figured that, with the bouffant hair like a nest and all the hairspray, the crown had ended up in the patient's hair, stuck in there unnoticed until a hairdresser combed it out and down the drain. Or, if she or he noticed it at all, took it to a pawnshop and bought a nice cruise to the Bahamas.

I was 43 when I started out in private practice as a Licensed Mental Health Counselor. I was green as a Florida palm. I wondered if I could sit for an entire hour with a client (yes). I wondered if I could be a help to people (probably). I wondered if I could collect money for this, since helping people seemed like something that should be done for free (a recurrent problem).

Fortunately, I was seeing my mentor Carole Leeds on a weekly basis to report on my professional progress. "I am seeing a young man who goes week after week without paying me," I told her. "What should I do?"

She stared thoughtfully at me. "You remind him that you have a contract and you ask if he is going to honor that contract."

That seemed pretty clear-cut. The next week I said those words to him and watched as his facial expression turned into that of a young sulky child and he squirmed in his chair.

"I'm *planning* to pay you," he said. "But my checkbook's in the car."

"I'll wait while you get it," I said, and did. He wrote me a check rather slowly. I never saw him again.

My first couple consisted of a woman who complained, "When I walk into the kitchen I bang my forehead on an open cabinet door. My husband keeps opening them and leaving them open."

I thought this rather trivial, but didn't say so out loud. The man sat there. *I'm wearing a halo*, his expression said.

Again I checked with my mentor, who suggested, "Ask him if he intends to shut the cabinet doors."

I thought *this* rather trivial, but didn't say so. The next week I asked him, "Do you intend to shut the cabinet doors?"

He appeared taken aback by the question. "I guess not," he said slowly.

His wife let out a huge sigh. "This marriage is over," she said. And just like that, it was.

It taught me that the greater part of a troubled relationship, like a glacier, is underneath where a person might not be able to see it, but where something like an open cabinet door could serve as metaphor for a problem.

And that I was very, very fortunate to have Carole as my guide.

✫ ✫ ✫

I'm reaching the end of my book and I have not told you enough about my parents and especially about my father, our Dad. At his funeral my sister Judy whispered to me, "We lived with a saint," and I agreed with her.

We never saw him angry or impatient. If he was (those are such human traits), he hid them from us. Even when Mom walked out into the snow in her nightgown, looking for a fish sandwich at McDonald's. Even when she put the coffee pot and the toaster in the bathtub in case of fire.

I saw him discouraged once and it changed my life. He worked as a senior master machinist at Fafnir Bearings in New Britain. One day when I was a young teenager he came home from work and slumped down on a kitchen chair.

"I was passed over," he told us. "I was supposed to be the head machinist—I certainly had the years of experience—". We all nodded. We knew his skills. "But they hired a kid right out of college. A youngster." A look passed across his eyes that I had never seen before, and I decided right then that I would go to college so that this would never have to happen to me.

I still don't know how it happened that I got my own bedroom. We had three bedrooms upstairs and my parents had had the downstairs "front room" that they used for a bedroom, for years. But suddenly my brothers were getting one bedroom, my sisters another, and I was to move into the third bedroom—a tiny one, but with windows on two walls.

I was beside myself with joy over my own territory. I had bunked with Judy for so many years! She wasn't tidy—she would wear my clean starched dresses and then step out of them at the end of the day, leaving them on the floor like wilted pathetic blossoms. I silently cheered when she grew taller than me and outgrew my clothes.

One day when I was nine, I took some birthday money and bought a lock at the Five and Ten. I nailed it to our bedroom door. Ha! Now she'd have to knock when she wanted to come in while I was playing with paper dolls.

My privacy lasted under an hour. "Let me in!" yelled Judy. "It's my room, too!"

I didn't answer. The next sound was of my irate mother pounding on the door. "Barbara! You let your sister *in!*"

I did. Some people got their fifteen minutes of fame. I got my fifteen minutes of privacy.

So for my new room I was allowed to pick out the wallpaper. I chose a pattern of pussywillows in yellow tones against a warm gray background.

My mother raised her eyebrows at my selection, and Dad set up a board for cutting and pasting the paper.

This was an afternoon I'll never forget, although I have no remembrance of our conversation—just that I had his attention, and even though people tried to get in, Dad said, "Don't come in and step on anything until we're done," and my siblings would sulk away back down the stairs and Dad and I would go back to measuring the pussywillow print.

With one bathroom and seven of us in the house after my grandparents died, there was never enough privacy. "There's no toilet paper in here!" Tommy would call through the bathroom door.

"Barbara," my mother would order," go to Rizzo's for a roll of toilet paper. Here's a dime."

"Can't you send someone else?" I would ask, my attention deep in a book.

If Dad were home, he'd get up from his chair with the lion arms and say, "I'll go"

Then we kids all wanted to go—walking to the store with Dad was an adventure! And we might be able to wheedle a piece of penny candy while we were with him.

"Bring me something, too!" came Tommy's muffled voice. "And toilet paper!"

When I was grown and had a dozen rolls of toilet paper stashed in my bathrooms, I asked my mother, "Why did you only have us buy one roll at a time?"

She looked at me as though I had asked something any toddler could comprehend.

"Why—If I bought more, you all would just *use* it," she said.

She gave Dad two dollars at a time to buy gas. She herself never drove and I thought Dad should be in charge of the gas money, since he was the driver.

We kids went with him when he went to buy gas. This was another adventure with him. He pumped his own gas.

"Dad, why does Mom only give your two dollars?" I asked one day.

"She's afraid if she gave me more, I'd run away from home," he joked.

But was it a joke? She was so dependent on him. He only went away overnight once in my growing-up years with them—fishing with some friends—and Mom was so scared to be alone that she got into my bed with me. I was twelve. I was annoyed that she couldn't take care of us instead of the other way around.

Once a man we didn't know came to the house. "Is Red here?" he said.

Red? Red Who? We kids wondered, and then realized he was talking about our red-haired Dad.

Our Dad knew men who called him "Red" at work! Suddenly he had another life other than the one of being our Dad!

He did have sandy-red hair. And freckles. Loads of freckles. He told us that when he was a boy at a camp, he'd been given an award for having the most freckles of anyone there.

Now I was a snooper. Curious, nosy, wanting to know more about the people who were raising me, I sneaked into their bedroom when I could and looked for—what? Evidence that Mom was not my real Mom? I did go through that stage.

Once I found a box of what I thought was chocolate candy, in a box marked "Ex-Lax". I don't know how much I ate. I craved chocolate, and this looked good to me. I also have blocked from my memory whatever happened the next day.

Chocolate! In first grade I walked to the center of Plainville with Dad and saw the heart-shaped displays of Valentine candy in the drugstore window.

"Please, Daddy," I begged. "please let me take a box of candy to my teacher."

I loved my first-grade teacher. I secretly believed she was my real mother and that someday she and Dad would admit it to me. But in the meantime there was chocolate.

Dad gave in to my pleadings and bought a small box of Valentine chocolates to give to my teacher. I showed off the box to everyone in the family. Fortunately it was wrapped in cellophane, so nobody could get to the candy. I saw my mother give a disdainful look to my father, but I didn't care.

I took the box of chocolates to my teacher, but—I was too shy to give it to her.

So I hid it in my raised-top desk, tore open the cellophane, sneaked pieces out, sure that no one could see me doing it, and ate them all myself.

"Barbara," my teacher said to me in a mild tone of voice, "all that candy is going to make you sick."

Maybe it did. Do all kids remember the start of something, but not the consequences?

Dad read the funny papers to us on Sunday mornings, before church. These were not what passes for Sunday comics today—these were big, oversized pages with larger than usual panels—Dick Tracy! Toonerville

Trollies! Little Orphan Annie! We'd spread them out on the floor and Dad would read them over our shoulders.

My life was saddened when I asked him to read to us one Sunday and he said, "You know how to read now, Barbara. You can do it yourself."

It wasn't the reading that gave me joy, I realized—it was *Dad* reading.

When I studied to be a therapist I wondered if perhaps my mother had a Borderline personality. She certainly had an ambivalence toward me that I never understood, until a family member told me that Mom had gotten tipsy once with a female neighbor, and had confessed that I was the child of someone else —"the brother of one of the men in the b and"—, and Dad had married her anyway.

"I think you might be half Italian, Barb," my brother John said to me after he overheard the women's conversation.

"Well," I said, trying to take in the enormity of this idea," that would explain why I love pasta."

Was all this true? The older I get, the less I care, unless there's some awful physical doom running in that Italian family. When I found out what Mom had said, I decided that no matter what (and I told him so with a hug), he was my real Dad and nobody else mattered. He neither confirmed nor denied the story, but John reported to me that he looked as though a burden had been lifted from him.

But Mom certainly had an ambivalence toward me. When I married and came home from college in my junior year to announce that I was pregnant, instead of congratulating me, she made an angry leap at me and wrapped her hands around my throat. Fortunately her female Swedish cousins were there at the time, and they pulled her off before I knew to be startled, saying, "Shame on you, Ruthie. Shame."

Did she have dreams for me that didn't include pregnancy? Or was I accidentally repeating her young life? I'll never know.

For their fiftieth anniversary my sister-in-law Pat and I took Mom to a department store to buy her a dress. It was then that I realized she was well into dementia, as she dutifully took everything we handed her to try on—and disrobed in the middle of the aisle. She kept calling, "Les, Les!" while we assured her that we'd take her right back to him.

"I wish you could have seen Dad," said my brother John when we got home, exhausted. "He sat in our pool in a big black inner tube and just enjoyed himself. 'First time in years I've had time to myself,' he kept saying."

Dad and I and our need for privacy, for territory just our own. I am indeed his daughter. In his sense of humor I am his daughter. In his church choir singing I am his daughter.

Dad drove us to Sunday School every week on the bad snowy winter days. We'd huddle in the old Ford, our breath materializing before us, while Dad showed us how to keep the choke and the throttle buttons pulled out. Then he'd put the metal crank into the hole in the front of the car and give the crank a twist. He had told us that if it jerked back, he could get hurt. We were relieved when the car started and he was all right.

By the time I was 18 and into Driver's Ed, we had a secondhand Buick. I took my first driving lesson and came home from school, pulling on Dad's arm to get us into the car and let me show him all I had learned.

We went to Norton Park, which was almost deserted at that time of day, and then I sat in the driver's seat with Dad by my side. I was so proud of myself!

Except I had not yet learned how to downclutch and when I decided to go around a sharp curve at about 10 miles per hour, I lost control of the big heavy car and rammed headfirst into a tree.

I sat there speechless. Dad got out of the car and examined it. One of the foglights had bent. He came back to the driver's side window. I started to get out, trying not to cry.

"No," he said, "you *need* to drive right now, or else you never will," and he had me drive home.

That's the kind of man he was. As I said, I never saw him angry, never heard him swear.

As for my mother, the enigmatic, emotions-pent-up, could-have-been-a-classical-pianist, and me—a miracle happened.

By then I was 25. My husband and I had twin daughters and another one just 16 months younger, all not yet in school. I was expecting again and I had the flu.

Limp in bed with a fever and with my husband out of town, I phoned my mother in desperation to come help me by watching the girls. I had never asked this of her before.

To my surprise she got a relative to drive her and as soon as she was inside our front door, I fell asleep.

I woke up to an unusual sound and I heaved myself to the upstairs bedroom window. Down in the yard in the snow my mother stood, with three snowsuited and booted girls, all of them laughing.

"Block-a-bloo!" my mother called, and toppled herself backward into the snow while the girls laughed so hard they had to sit down. "*Block-a-bloo!*"

She had never played like this with me! This was a mother I did not know!

My daughters yelled, "Block-a-bloo!" after her and fell down into the snow, copying her. They kept laughing and she kept making snow angels of herself.

I call this a miracle. One silly made-up word washed away all the resentments and pain I had felt toward her and I was *never* able to get those negative emotions back again.

So I've decided— when I get to heaven and see her I am going to yell "Block-a-bloo!" and we'll both laugh and fall into a cloudbank together.

✲ ✲ ✲

Surely the Presence of the Lord is in this Place

As I wait in the Atlanta airport for Mitch to get our rental car I suddenly hear a flapping, pattering sound, as though someone has set free thousands of birds.

I look around. There is little conversation. The sound continues— ah!— the passengers in the waiting area are applauding a long line of military men and women who are about to board planes to take them out of the country.

What young faces these soldiers have! The heartfelt applause continues as more and more people begin to clap. No shouts of triumph, no "hurrah!"s fill the air—simply the sound of hundreds of strangers, their politics set aside, applauding as one.

My eyes fill with tears. Son Jon is in Afghanistan and surely he was applauded in this way, too. I think this is what angels must sound like, their mighty wings beating as they bear Good News from God to people.

We are here for Mitch's fiftieth class reunion at Emory Dental School. I know few of the people, since most of the men have been married fifty years and have known each other on a long-term basis. Twelve have died. Almost all the rest of the 53 graduates are here with their wives.

(1958 was the last year at Emory to graduate only men. The next year there was one woman, and then every year more, so that now female dentists equal males around the country.)

Each man gets up to say a few words. Some have retired; some (like Mitch) are still working full time. To a man they say the same thing: "I love this profession. If I had to do it again, I'd still choose dentistry."

The ones who have retired say as a chorus: "I miss the people." The patients—they miss the connections with their patients.

We go back to our room and Mitch turns on TV to see the rest of a basketball game. There has been some sort of furor in downtown Atlanta where he is to go tomorrow for more dental meetings. The announcers are reluctant to call the destruction a tornado, but it turns out this is what it was—the first tornado to hit the center of Atlanta in the history of the city. We see windows blown out in the CNN building where we stood a day before. And miraculously, with all the thousands of spectators in the GeorgiaDome for the basketball game, there are no casualties, even though part of the roof blows off.

The next day I see on TV coverage of people in a small now-devastated area of Atlanta ("Cabbagetown") who have all banded together to help and feed each other, even as the Red Cross and Salvation Army show up.

Mitch has gone downtown for the dental meetings, which he finds have been canceled due to the extensive damage. So he decides to go to the aquarium nearby. Inside a tour group of people surround him. One woman says, "We're from Dauphin Way Baptist Church in Mobile."

Mitch, astounded, says, "That was my church there when I was young. Maybe we were in the same Sunday School class!"

They exchange names and find they have friends in common from fifty years ago, and the woman is a friend of his second cousin. "Her husband just died two weeks ago," the woman says—and this is how Mitch finds out about a relative he has known from his younger life.

As we get ready to leave the next day (Palm Sunday), at the airport we discover an extensive collection of immense stone sculptures by artists in Zimbabwe. The energy exuding from these massive, life-affirming carvings of African families is such that I <u>have</u> to touch, to get the stone's life beneath the skin of my hand. I need more than my eyes and my heart to help me here. The creativity takes my breath away.

I hear the pattering as I join my hand to the stones. I still believe it sounds like angels' wings, hushed as prayer, united as prayer.

2008

✫ ✫ ✫

Christmas Mysteries

Halfway to Christmas and I'm tired of shopping. I wonder if people who out-and-out <u>love</u> shopping ever get weary from shopping.

I'm tired of the crumpled piece of paper in my pocket that was once a tidy list. Now it has crossed-out names (as I've bought the recipients their gifts) and erasures and is mostly creases. My jaws ache from clenching my teeth while reading price tags.

The cashier at the checkout counter appears to be my age —71—and she is still amiable after standing on her feet all day. "I think I have the correct change," I say, pawing through my purse in a way that my grown children chide me about, since it makes me look like (to them) an old fussy lady.

"Take your time," she answers. What a wonderful thought—permission to take my time!

I unlock the car door, toss my packages onto the back seat, turn on the radio with its Christmas music, and head for home, singing, "Do you hear what I hear?" with an ageless Perry Como.

I am almost beyond it before my mind registers what I have just seen. I turn the car around to take another look: it's a <u>tree</u>, a Christmas tree! Thrown out beside the road <u>before</u> Christmas! It's a live one, large, deep green and forest-scented as only a real tree can be, and it glints in the late afternoon sun with a few strands of silvery icicles. The sparkle is what first caught my eye.

I can't stay here, can't tell whose house the tree belonged to—traffic is building up behind me.

I drive toward home, musing. What if the couple in one of the houses had had a fight about something and one of them got really angry while trimming the tree and yanked it down, hurled it out for the trash men?

Or what if, like an O. Henry story, a couple had each bought a tree; and laughing with the joyousness of surprising each other, they had tossed a coin and decided which one to keep?

Or what if they'd suddenly decided to go visit relatives in New England as a treat for themselves and had junked the tree as they were packing?

One thing was certain. I didn't want to know the truth. I would rather have fun saying, "What if—?" than know for sure. Since I have been young I have known this—people could have given me an empty box all wrapped up and I would have had a grand time guessing what the box might contain without ever opening it; the opposite of doubting Thomas, who had to see the reality of wounds for himself before he would believe.

Once my youngest son, then a college student, told me, "We had a tree in our fraternity house and I was the last to leave. So I put the tree outside, hoping someone would pick it up and have a happy Christmas with it."

So now I hope that someone following me while I was singing in the car would see the tree, stop and haul the heavy evergreen into his car, driving it home to surprise his family while he sang the same carols.

The whole mystery of Christmas is that nobody can adequately explain it and I want it that way. It is a <u>holy</u> mystery: a young teenager tells her betrothed that God has gotten her pregnant. Her betrothed defies the community and marries her. He has weird dreams that tell him her story is true. After the baby's birth they flee and the wicked king they leave behind orders all the young children to be killed. Three wise men come to visit the baby because they have been led by a star—this is the stuff of fiction stories, not of a time that split the world into B.C.(Before Christ) and A.D. (Anno Domini—in the year of our Lord).

At Christmas I want us once more to admire the Gift that has been handed us. I want us to rejoice that God wrapped a gift for us that we get to open and fully understand in heaven.

Blessings this Christmas as we revere this most holy of mysteries— EMMANUEL—GOD WITH US.

2008

✫ ✫ ✫

Easter 2007

"Now the green blade riseth from the buried grain,
Wheat that in the dark earth many days hath lain;
Love lives again, that with the dead has been;
Love is come again like wheat that springeth green."

John Macleod Campbell Crum (1872-1958).

The above words are verse 1 from hymn 204 in the 1982 hymnal. Usually only a choir sings this hymn, because its tempo is quick and its melody unusual for a church congregation used to the more familiar Easter hymns. However, it is a beautiful hymn with a metaphor that any gardener understands.

When I was a youngster attending the Episcopal Church of Our Saviour (yes, the British spelling!) in Plainville, Connecticut, our minister Mr. Frye (they were not priests then and they were not called "Father") would hold a special Easter service for us Sunday School children.

I sat and tried not to covet the well-to-do girls who marched in primly with their new Easter dresses, hats, gloves and shiny little purses containing a quarter and a lace handkerchief. My younger sister Judy and I usually wore straw hats that looked as though someone had sat on them first; and this was true, since we had two rowdy younger brothers.

We stared at the front of the little church. Between the divided choir stalls, in front of the altar, had been placed a simple five-foot high, handmade, dark-stained wooden cross. It was pocked with many holes.

We kids were then invited to come choose a flower from a huge vase—daffodils, hyacinth, tulips in various pastel shades—and poke our flower's stem through a hole in the cross. The vision of that cross before and after the flower adornment still brings a catch to my throat when I picture it in my memory.

The perfume of the cut flowers filled the altar area. Mr. Frye then told a story about how the cross had been transformed from dead to living.

But I could hardly sit still! I could smell what was coming up the aisle from behind me before I ever saw it—a heavy box carried by two ushers—a box full of potted flowers. The marigold scent was overwhelmed by the pungent odor of fresh earth. After the long cold dark winter, that heady, earthy smell burst into the church, all but shouting that without a doubt Easter was here and spring was on its way; there was no way for me to separate spring and Easter.

I marveled: where had this earth come from? I didn't know about plant nurseries and to me this was a miracle—fresh dirt where outside everything was still covered with snow and slush.

We children were then given a plant to take home and put into the ground once the weather got a little warmer. I hung back after the service, pulling at Judy's sleeve to make her stay, too. I knew if there were leftover plants we could get an extra one. The scent of the dirt made me bold.

How marvelous that we have Easter and spring to celebrate at the same time! Jesus Who died and was put into the earth (the tomb) and rose from it gives us the undeniable message that we are also to rise and meet Him ourselves, face to face.

And if summer, fall and winter are of the world, surely spring and the time of new growth is of heaven.

> "When our hearts are wintry, grieving, or in pain,
> Thy touch can call us back to life again,
> Fields of our hearts that dead and bare have been:
> Love is come again like wheat that springeth green."

verse 4, hymn 204

2007

✹ ✹ ✹

"God has no Curiosity"

"What's this book?" says Mitch, holding up a book from beside my chair.

I look up from a book I am reading at the dining room table.. "It's about the Plague and how a flea infestation wiped out a third of Europe in the 500s A.D. Don't take the book mark out; I'm still reading it."

"But you're reading <u>that</u> one."

"This one's fiction. That one isn't."

"So is that the one from upstairs?"

"No. That's a Scott Peck book that I'm re-reading. I read it several years ago and I'm going through it again."

"<u>Three</u> books. How can you keep track in your mind, reading three books at a time? Why don't you read one at a time and then start another? That's what I do."

This isn't the time to mention the Pogo book in my bathroom.

One of the greatest gifts I ever received as a child was when my friend Sally's mother took us to the public library and helped us fill out the paperwork for library cards. My own library card!

I looked around hungrily, the way Willie Sutton must have cased a bank. The children's library was in the basement of the old square stone building. Going down the worn granite stairs in the summer I would feel a welcome blast of cooler air, even if I first had to move past the glass cases of dead stuffed birds and their eggs to get to the treasure of books.

My talisman of a card in hand in case the prune-faced upstairs librarian stared at me, I got bolder and dared to go into the main library on the first floor. I found my first teenage books there (they were fluffy things with advice on how to wear makeup and get a boyfriend), and then fell into adult books of short stories, written with such muscular power that I yearned to do that, too. I could recite some of the stories to you today, the force of the world of grownup writing impressed me so.

And another flight up! —behind the forbidding librarian curved a set of black metal stairs to the little gallery above. I learned that if I showed my card and said, "May I go upstairs, please?", she would frown, stop stamping book inserts, give an examining look at my hands—clean enough?— and open the little wooden gate that separated her from us readers. I always walked quietly past her to give her no reason to refuse me entrance.

Upstairs were the art books. It was silent there. Usually I was alone except for one buzzing fly and I could sit on the floor and enjoy these oversized books.

Further on, I discovered by accident a series of large hard-bound music books for piano. <u>Music</u>! In a <u>library</u>! Trying to hide my excitement, I would check out one music book a week, running home to go through the pages and practice on our old upright piano.

I worked my way up from beginners to the most difficult. All I could do was study those pages—they were too advanced for me then.

My mother looked over my shoulder. "Ah, 'Rustle of Spring'", she said. "I played that at my high school recital." She edged me off the piano stool and sat down, her fingers flashing over the keys. For the first time in my life, I was aware of how talented she was as a pianist.

(Many years later I found the same series of music books at a library sale here in Melbourne. "My old friends!" I smiled, elated, and bought them on the spot. I still have trouble playing "Rustle of Spring".)

Which leads me to the book of fiction I am reading. The author states, "God has no curiosity."

Of course He does, I protest, and she goes on: "He has no curiosity because curiosity assumes there is something He does not know, yet He knows all."

(I read this passage to Mitch and then say, "Does God wear a wristwatch?" He laughs and says, joining me, "Sure—a Rolex." I say, "I think He wears a Timeless.")

But if God has no curiosity, what do we do about the sticky subject of Free Will? If He knows all that is going to happen, we then are nothing but pre-programmed people.

I add this to my list of questions to ask God when I see Him, even though I sense the answer won't matter then.

So—I decide that curiosity is a "human" word which means we are trying and learning something new. That makes curiosity a great gift from God to us.

I hope the last thing I lose in this life is my gift of curiosity, especially about the next world. I'll bet there's a gigantic library there with no need for librarian or card.

Or bifocals.

2009

✯ ✯ ✯

From the Head to the Heart

There's a story about two monks who belonged to an order that forbade, among other things, the touching of women. So they were nonplussed when they came to a raging river on one of their walks—beside the river was a woman who pleaded with them to help her get across.

She was slight of build and would have been unable to keep her footing, so the first monk picked her up and carried her across the water, to the obvious disapproval of the second monk, who spent the next week chastising the other.

The first monk bore the lectures quietly, but finally said, "Brother—I carried that woman and it took me ten minutes to do so. You have been carrying her for the past seven days."

I played recently as a substitute organist and was given the list of hymns. One of them was to the tune of "My Country, 'tis of Thee", but with different words (look in the hymnal at hymns 716 and 717), and I gnashed my teeth over this, knowing that most of the congregation was older and would enjoy singing the words they had once learned in elementary school.

I couldn't get my frustration at playing "the wrong words" from my head until I finally remembered the monks and said to myself, "Barb, playing this hymn will take all of four minutes. You have been carrying it for over a week."

Then that Sunday the priest preached, "Get over yourself and quit getting caught up in all the details." Well, that certainly was a sermon for me!

He read the Comfortable Words (and you former Latin I students know that "comfortable" means "with strength", not "cushy soft")—"Come unto me, all ye that are heavy laden,"—bring your burden to God. Note this well: you need to make that first move.

"—and I will refresh you"—just as nothing refreshes like a cool drink of water on a hot Florida day.

The words come after the confession in the Rite One service, so that we can unburden from a "head trip" (rationalization—"It wasn't my fault", "anybody would have done the same thing", "what do you expect when I'm tired", etc.) to a "heart trip" ("God, I'm mad/scared/sad/anxious/frustrated" etc.).

This "heart to heart" is a sharing with God, of dropping the pretense that we are in charge and can control things, to the realization that we don't have to, and God is waiting to take on the load we have been struggling to carry.

Then, after giving it to God, don't pick it up again! Don't keep carrying it as the second monk did. This has to be the hardest part of setting a problem down—to let it go.

"—and I will give you rest." What a powerful reward for unburdening ourselves to God!

What are you carrying that God is yearning to carry for you? Be as the faithful monk: lay it down. Lay it down. And stop yourself when you try to pick it up again. God is already in charge—amen!

2009

Hot Springs

Mitch and I are following a narrow, stony trail up a mountain in Hot Springs, Arkansas. The sign at the bottom of the trail read "A short but rather steep climb to the top and to the tower."

It is not short. It *is* steep. There are blankets of poison ivy on either side of the trail, and covering the tall trees from the bottom, making it impossible to stop and lean upon one while we catch a breath.

Our plane landed in Arkansas in August less than two hours ago. We found a sandwich shop and after lunch Mitch noticed a park across the street. "Let's go over there," he said, crossing the street ahead of me.

Then he saw the trail and decided he had to try it. Reluctantly I went with him, not wanting to leave him alone.

So now, unprepared for hiking, I am carrying my heavy purse, a jacket, and a small bottle of water. I am wearing loafers. I am also wearing a white cotton shirt. This will prove handy for wiping my sweaty, dirty face as we plod upward.

I mentioned it is August. It is 2:00 pm. Nobody knows where we are. My cell phone needs to be recharged. We will be attending a psychological seminar tomorrow with some of my favorite gurus of Transactional Analysis. I have planned this trip since January.

At the least I could spend it scratching poison ivy legs. At the worst, one of us could slide all the way back to the bottom of the mountain and spend time staring at the ceiling of the Hot Springs hospital.

"I saw—I saw—," Mitch puffs as we climb, "—in the newspaper at the lunchroom that Al Capone used to come here with his cronies. They'd reserve the entire fourth floor of the hotel where we're going to stay."

"I'll bet they never climbed a mountain," I answer. I know I have to save my breath. I am silently praying, "Lord, don't let us die here on a mountain outside of Little Rock," and I am humming "Nearer My God To Thee" as I trudge onward. I can see Mitch's back, about 20 paces ahead of me. He's not exactly bounding like a gazelle. We are easily the oldest tourists on this deserted trail.

In a clearing we look down at the town. There's our hotel, way far down there. We've been climbing for about an hour now. I want to know who wrote the sign "Short but Steep".

I can see the tower up above us. And suddenly we are out of the woods and crossing a road—a road! We could have driven up here! In an air-conditioned car! I am now ahead of Mitch and I look back to say "I told you so", but he is sitting on a large rock, catching his breath.

I give him the last of the water from the little bottle. "I'll see how much farther," I say. He nods, but can't talk. I've been working in the yard the past month, for a few hours each day, and apparently this has given me more stamina. I start up the last part of the trail, giving myself marching orders: "one-two-three-four, two-two-three-four." I call down to Mitch: "Only 83 steps!"

There is no response. I retrace my steps and he is still sitting, trying to catch his breath. Now I am worried. I feel like Bambi's father, urging, "Get up, Bambi! Get up!"

With effort Mitch makes it inside the tower, where the reception area is air-conditioned. "Are you okay to go on?" I ask. He nods yes, so we get into an elevator that takes us up to top and a lookout, some 80 feet higher than the top of the mountain.

Mitch rests against a wall. I look at all the placards around the inside of the lookout wall, but can't concentrate. I am wondering how we will get down, and I decide I will ask any handy stranger for a lift in his/her car. The view is breath-taking, but I am more concerned about Mitch's breath.

Back in the lobby I notice a cold drink machine, and Mitch buys a Gatorade. He feels better as soon as he starts drinking it, replacing his electrolytes. I am thinking about football players and band players who have to practice in this kind of heat. It seems like cruel and unusual punishment at this point.

Full of Gatorade, Mitch is ready to climb down the mountain. This proves much easier than getting up it. In 20 minutes we are at the bottom and limping toward the hotel. My shirt is wet and grimy. Our faces are fiery-red. My only prayer is "Thank you, Lord, for getting us down safely!"

I stop on the sidewalk and look up to the tower, far away in the distance now. We were just up there!

Next time I'll take the rental car and leave Mitch to walk if he wants.

He is reading a sign. "Look, Barb—here's a different trail—" .

2008

✯ ✯ ✯

The $3.69 Blouse

I am in Goodwill when I hear the soft under-the-breath swearing. The woman behind me at the racks is not using the Lord's name in vain, so I am amused, not offended.

She catches my eye. She is perhaps in her sixties, with a gap between her two upper front teeth. Her tight curls are starting to go gray. "I found this great blouse here last week, but I didn't have the money to pay for it, and now it's gone."

She holds up a white blouse. "Just like this one, only in a large size." She continues to shuffle through the circular rack of white and tan blouses, starting up the swearing again.

"Just when you found something you like, too," I say. "Isn't that always the way," she says, and we smile together.

Inside I am in tears. The blouse would have cost her $3.69, and she had to spend that money for something else. I am humbled listening to her.

"What I do is take what I want and put it in the men's section," I tell her. Her eyes light up. "What an idea! I'll do that next time. No way somebody's gonna find a blouse <u>there</u>."

We move to other racks and I go to the book section. I'm looking for a CD copy of Disney's "Song of the South", but without much hope—the movie was wrongfully considered racist and was withdrawn from circulation years ago.

Instead I find a cream pitcher to replace one I had broken and as I head to the front register I stop beside another rack of clothing; and there to my surprise is the blouse the woman was looking for!

I glance around and recognize her. "Look!" I say, holding up the blouse.

"How did you remember?" she says, seemingly astounded that someone would do that.

Now here's the tough part: I want with every fiber of my being, to <u>buy</u> that blouse for her. I am searching inside myself for a reason I can give her when she says, "It looks pinky, not white."

So we all study the blouse and we agree that someone might have washed it with something pink, and a little bleach would bring out the white again. "And if it doesn't and you leave the tag on," suggests the woman at the register, "you can bring it back and get a refund."

The buyer decides that's fine and for me the moment when I could have offered to pay for the blouse is gone. We have, though, for the moment in time, become buddies.

And now a day later I think of what I could have said: "I have been given a blessing today and I want to pass it on." It would have been that simple. And all the time I was thinking of how to save the woman's pride I was thinking of myself and how I might be embarrassed if I embarrassed her.

I want to tell her, "I've been there—I know the choking feeling of not having enough money. I know how it is to search for soda bottles to redeem at the store so my youngest son could buy bait and go fishing. I know how it is to be a waitress and earn quarters in tips so my children can have lunch money. I know!"

Oh, Lord, I know. Let me be charitable with the next person I meet. Let them see You reflected in me.

2012

✡ ✡ ✡

Three Gifts

One: When I was in third grade we each drew the name of a classmate and bought a 25 cent Christmas gift for that child. The gift to me was a lovely little fake china prancing horse and I had set it on my desk to admire it when some boys, full of sugary treats, raced around the room, knocked my horse to the floor and broke it.

The teacher, out of patience by then, chastised the boys and made one of them give me his gift. It was a balsa airplane and I didn't want to take it. Our family was poor, but I had a feeling this was the only present my male classmate was going to get for Christmas. I was forced to take the airplane home and my father mended the horse. I never looked at the horse again without seeing that boy's crestfallen face as he handed me his plane.

Two: The next Christmastime we kids in our family earned some coins for gifts by doing chores, and we four siblings headed for the Five and Ten Cent store downtown to buy presents.

Buying for my two younger brothers was easy: a ten cent comic book each, rolled into a tube and wrapped so that they could use it as a horn and toot through it as a kind of extra free present—what a clever idea, I praised myself.

My sister, a year younger than me, was harder to buy for, because everything I saw for her I wanted for <u>me</u>. So I finally decided on a little set of doll house furniture (ignoring the fact that <u>I</u> was the one who had the doll house, not Judy), wrapped it and labeled it with her name.

Then a day later I picked a fight with her and, convinced I was justified, went to the wrapped package, removed her name from the box and wrote mine on it instead.

I forgot all about it until Christmas morning, when I got an extra gift and she got none from me. I still see her face as she searched through the crushed wrapping paper on the floor, looking to find— what I had already opened and was staring at with a mounting sense of having done wrong.

Embarrassed, I dared not speak up. My parents, busy that day, didn't notice. Judy was too quiet to complain and this added to my remorse.

Three: Do you remember the old TV sitcom "Father Knows Best"? One episode still stands out for me, then a young teenager: Bud, the oldest son (and a teenager too), was given some money from someone outside the family. His father wanted him to put most of it in the bank, but Bud was determined to spend it all, since it had all come to him.

When the father saw how stubborn Bud was being, he said, "All right, son. But with one stipulation: you must spend it all on yourself, and <u>none</u> of it on anyone else."

Well, (there had to be a catch to this, but what could it be? I wondered, watching the show) Bud thought this was a grand idea and started making plans for his money. Then he wanted to treat his friends to a soda and realized he couldn't. He sadly and with insight came to the conclusion that a gift kept to oneself is not as good as a gift shared.

So by now we're buying our gifts and then will be into Epiphany, the time when the Wise Men appeared with their treasures.

We are told they shared their treasures gladly. It must have been an odd sight indeed: three men dressed like nobility, kneeling before a baby and his young parents, marveling at what had brought them to this place and at this time in their lives. A baby! Who bows to an unknown <u>baby</u>? There's a miracle in itself.

As I write this, a Cub Scout in a blue uniform has just picked up a plastic bag of canned food that I placed on the front porch. The Scouts had left empty bags in the neighborhood and they have come back to pick up the bags.

He doesn't see me smiling at his earnest young face. His mother waits at the end of our driveway to make sure he's safe. What lesson he must be learning about strangers who reach out to other strangers in need!

I believe one of God's gifts is that He has "hard-wired" us to share—sharing is built into our very cells. Just imagine, like Bud, not ever being allowed to share our time, our talents, our treasures, our lives.

So—my next act is to call my sister and apologize for the doll house furniture. She is a passionate art teacher to physically and emotionally challenged children and is one of the best sharers I know.

Have I stirred up any memories of someone you need to share with? Oh, I hope so.

2009

✲ ✲ ✲

Touching Others' Lives

"Whatever you do will be insignificant, but it is very important that you do it."

Gandhi

If you have heard this story before, no matter—it is worth retelling:

A female elementary teacher who was retired decided she wanted to donate her time and talents to others. And so she offered to help children with their homework assignments while they had to be in the hospital.

The first day she entered the hospital as a volunteer, she was given a young boy's name and was told to "teach him his multiplication and division tables". She found his room and to her surprise it was in the burn unit; worse, her first student was heavily medicated, with burns over much of his body.

"Why would they give me such a task?" she wondered to herself, but went to his bedside. "I'm a teacher, and I'm here to teach you multiplication and division," she told him in a matter-of-fact tone, to hide her nervousness.

He seemed startled, but together they spent the next hour on arithmetic and she promised she would be back the next day to study with him some more.

The nurses somberly shook their heads toward the boy's room as she left. "He must be very bad off," she puzzled to herself.

The next day the same nurses greeted her with enthusiasm. "What did you do for him?" they said. "We'd given up hope, and yet here he is, sitting up and looking forward to seeing you again."

The teacher hurried into the room and spent a cheerful hour with the boy. Then as she left, she asked him with curiosity," What made such a difference in you between yesterday and today?"

"Well," he said, "when they sent me a teacher to help me learn multiplication and division, I figured <u>somebody</u> knew I was going to get better and go back home and then back to school, or why were they concerned about a simple thing like arithmetic?"

So here's a heavenly mystery: we are called on to help others without even knowing if we will make a difference. (Jesus said, "Do this to the least of my brethren and you are doing it to me"). We seem to be "hard-wired" by God to help others. And helping means starting out from some kind of gratefulness to God for our existence. The saddest people appear to be those who surround themselves with things, yet don't know how to share or do something for someone else.

Scott Peck says that all "Godfulness/prayerfulness" springs from a spirit of feeling grateful.

Three young men broke into our home last year and burglarized it. They were caught soon after. Two of them had police records and the third was new to this. He was a younger, small skinny kid and they used him to get into small bathroom windows and open the doors for them.

I was asked if I could speak on his behalf. "He won't last a day in prison," the lawyer for the State told me. "If you could only see how little he is—"

In court I thought he was 12 years old. I wonder how much he had been teased in school about his height and weight and lack of muscles. Shaking (the way we all do when a police car suddenly puts on its blue flashing lights near us while we are driving), I approached the judge.

"I don't know this young man at all, "I said, while he stood beside his mother and looked at the floor, "but isn't there some community service he could do instead of going to prison? Could he maybe go around to schools and talk about what it's like to go outside the law?"

"You don't know him at all?"

"No, your honor."

"He broke into your home."

"Yes, sir."

The judge addressed the young man. "Do you realize what this woman is doing for you, asking for mercy for you after what you put her and others through?" The boy nodded, still not looking at me.

"All right," the judge said. "I'm putting you on probation for five years. You can't step out of line even once or you'll be finding yourself in prison. Do you understand?" Again he nodded.

This was in March. I puzzled over what to do in addition, and decided to send him a Christmas card with a note asking him to let me know how he is doing.

There was no response. I prayed for him anyway.

2008

A Little Fork History For Us Folks

As you dig into the turkey and then the pumpkin pie this Thanksgiving, take a look at the fork you hold in your hand. Then consider Da Vinci's "The Last Supper". Aha! There are no forks on the table.

Leonardo Da Vinci wasn't just striving for historical accuracy. If he had painted a fork he would have been inviting heresy charges. At the end of the 11th century, Italian Cardinal Peter Damian had castigated the fork as un-Christian. The cardinal called it an "excessive delicacy" and an immoral tool, fit only for courtesans and Persians.

The problem was that the fork had originated outside Christian Europe. The first known fork arrived in Europe in the 11th century, in the baggage of a Byzantine princess. The princess scandalized her new Venetian in-laws by eating with a two-pronged golden utensil.

The cardinal ruled that "God in his wisdom has provided man with natural forks—his fingers." After all, he noted, the Devil carried a pitchfork. When the princess died of a mysterious disease, Damian claimed for all to hear that the cause had been her blasphemous use of the fork.

However, outrageously fashionable Italians began living dangerously by using forks. For centuries, however, the fork remained an affectation even among the aristocracy. It was used only for foods in heavy sauces and was often shared with a tablemate.

At the end of the 16th century the conservative French aristocrat Montaigne noted, with pride for his disregard of fashion, that he "made little use" of the fork while dining. The British, skeptical of anything coming from the Continent of Europe, kept using their God-given fingers until well into the 17th century. (The famous eating scene from the movie "Tom Jones" comes to mind.)

The little Persian utensil never became popular in the Far East. Most East Asians valued the comparative delicacy and precision of chopsticks. Early forks—flat and two-pronged—to them seemed clumsy. When the Chinese saw European missionaries eat with knives and forks they derided the custom as "practicing butchery at the table."

Gradually as the fork became used more widely, the utensil as art came into being with the lengthening and subtle bowing of the handle, the increase in the number of tines, and the addition of graceful curves and elegant engraving.

So here's one more thing to be thankful for as you eye that second piece of pie—you can down it without having to worry that you are using the Devil's pitchfork.

Enjoy your Thanksgiving dinner and use as many different kinds of forks as are placed before you! (With apologies to the one having to do the dishes.) You are in no danger of being called a heretic and cast out of the Church.

2008

I loved working here! Melbourne Times newspaper.

Ending with a Laugh

What I like about writing is *Having Written*. Any writer will understand this.

I had parts in plays from the time I moved to Florida. It was fun to get out away from the house and the kids, and be someone else. I couldn't do it now; I'm afraid I can't memorize lines any more and there aren't many roles for 76-year-old women, either.

When was the last time you saw Meryl Streep take the part of a college girl?

One wonderful summer Indian River Players, the little theater I belonged to under the direction of the talented David Beyer, held a one-act play contest. I went to the evening of three one-acts and I said to myself, "*I* could do this!"

So I wrote a play and submitted it the next year. And my play was selected to be performed. Oh, the joy of creating characters and then of seeing them onstage, saying my words and making them come to life!

So I wrote the next year and the next and was selected each time.

I wondered if my name was getting me selected, so I chose a pseudonym—and I was selected! I've kept the plaques on my walls wherever I've lived.

Then I sent one to the New England Workshop and it was selected, given a second place award. You have no idea how this boosts the ego of a divorced and newly-remarried housewife and even newer grandmother.

The New England group met that year in Providence, Rhode Island. I met Kitty Carlisle, the still-beautiful widow of Moss Hart (one of my favorite playwrights). There was a reading of my play and for the first time I heard people laugh. *At my dialogue! They laughed!* I thought I had written a drama.

During the question and answer period afterward, "I have to ask why people laughed at my lines," I said. "I didn't think they were funny."

"We were laughing," an audience member said, "because they were so true to life and we could see ourselves in them."

Oh. That was a *good* thing.

✡ ✡ ✡

I have not written into this book the junky things I went through and grew stronger from. We all have our own junky stuff. Inevitably I found that writing about my junk is boring. What matters is what we do with it.

There's an 80's saying: "God does not make junk." So here's my quick view of God, satan, and heaven. It could be inscribed on a postcard:

When we die we face God and Jesus Christ and in the face of *all* that overwhelming love, we say, "Yes!" Yes, You are in charge. Yes, you know me inside and out. Yes, I have no room for pride, self-doubt, fear, shame, when I look into those glorious Faces and am surrounded by all that infinite Love.

It does not seem fashionable for Episcopalians to talk about Satan. Satan is too out of fashion for any church that can boast a pipe organ and a balanced budget. But I believe satan is the original one who looked into the Face of God and said "No!" No, I am just as good as you. Or better.

So I believe that those few people bound for hell are they who in death look into God's wholly loving Face and still say "No!"

Satan can only live in denial and destroy, not create. If it created, it would have to acknowledge God's glory. So hell (as C.S. Lewis says and I agree) is so small you can barely make it out. One of the lies satan whispers is that hell is so huge. But it's miniscule. And boring. And junk. With no healthy sense of humor, no gratitude.

✯ ✯ ✯

There was a tragic accident in a coal mine some years ago and the people of the community gathered to try and catch sight of their loved ones coming from the shaft.

A woman said to the local pastor, "Where was God, Pastor? *Where was God?*"

"Right here with us," was the answer. "In the midst of us, here with us. Now. Here."

✯ ✯ ✯

I love the approach of the late humorist Erma Bombeck, who said, "When I enter heaven I want to be as I am—overweight, hair mussed, lipstick on my teeth—and I want to face God and say, *"What a glorious ride!"*

So I want to end this book with humor. I have a favorite anecdote from over the years, and also a newly-acquired one. Take your pick. Add your own:

(1) A young woman boarded a plane and sat down next to an older, well-dressed woman who was wearing an enormous diamond ring on one of her fingers.

""Excuse me," said the young woman enviously, "I couldn't help noticing your ring."

"Oh, yas," answered the older woman. "Between da Hope Diamond and da Liz Taylor Diamond dere's dis one—da *Klapotnick* Diamond."

"Oh, my," gasped the young woman. "What I wouldn't give to have a diamond like that—!"

"No!" yelled the older woman. "No, you don't! Dere's a coise! A *coise* comes wit' da Klapotnick Diamond!"

"Oh, my goodness, a curse!—what kind of curse?"

"*Mister* Klapotnick."

✭ ✭ ✭

(2) A very wealthy man was determined to take it all with him when he died, so he called upon God to make a bargain. "Just one suitcase, that's all I want," he told God.

"You don't need a suitcase in heaven," said God. "But for you—okay."

"And I want to put anything I want in it," pressed the rich man

"Okay, okay," said God. "You sure know how to wheel and deal."

The rich man thought what he could bring with him—money was his first and only idea—but paper? And what kind—the dollar, the pound, the yen?

He decided on gold bullion and weighted down as large a suitcase as he could manage with the gold. Soon after that he died. He didn't worry—he had his suitcase full of gold.

At the gate to heaven St. Peter stopped him. "No suitcases allowed."

"God told me it was okay."

"Well—all right—but I need to inspect the contents."

St Peter opened the suitcase and stepped back. "Pavement? You brought *pavement?*"

✮ ✮ ✮

(3) One more that I just heard: A man in a fancy restaurant ordered a steak dinner. When it arrived, he said irritably to the waiter, "You have your thumb on my steak."

The waiter replied, "That's to keep it from falling off again."

Your turn.

Addendum: How I got my last name—when I divorced, at age 75, I went online, looking for a name that began with "B" and was unusual. There's a site called "howmanyofmearethere.com" and it was here that I discovered "Bayley". There are only 1283 of us in the U.S. And that's not too many relatives to keep track of. If you are a "Bayley", let me know. I love my new name. I'd enjoy meeting you.

Barbara Bayley is a church organist at Holy Trinity Episcopal Church in Melbourne, Florida. She moved from Connecticut to Florida and has lived in the Sunshine State for 50 years.

She has five children—Liz, Caroline, Diana, Jon and Chris; seven grandchildren— Jennifer, Michael, Rick, another Michael, April, Stacey, and Jonathan; and eight great-grandchildren. And of course her friend The Cat.

Her first book, "I could Always be a Waitress" was published under the name

BJ Radcliffe.

She welcomes comments about her books and hopes this one will give people ideas about writing their own histories.

Have a glorious ride!

You can write her at

b12bayley@cfl.rr.com

Made in the USA
Charleston, SC
22 December 2016